Given to

Lincoln Christian

College and Seminary

by

Dr. William Jessee

2/20/82

The Church
That Takes on Trouble

The Church That Takes on Trouble

JAMES AND MARTI HEFLEY

David C. Cook Publishing Co.
ELGIN, ILLINOIS—WESTON, ONTARIO
LA HABRA, CALIFORNIA

David C. Cook Publishing Co., Elgin, IL 60120
Printed in the United States of America
Library of Congress Catalog Number: 76-6579
ISBN: 0-912692-95-2

*To all of the people whose names
are not mentioned in this book,
who also gave themselves to the
ministry of LaSalle St. Church.*

Contents

Appendixes

8

Foreword

This story is as old as church history. It's the story of a church desperately trying to find itself at a difficult time in history, and of its relationship to its mother church and the institutions around it.

No doubt the story has been and will be repeated—a story of adapting to change, responding to human needs, determining priorities, and simply being the church in the world. The '60s were years of devastating instability, and LaSalle Street Church, as well as its parent, Moody Memorial Church, felt the pressures around them and the tensions within them.

We have asked to write this foreword to demonstrate the unity that exists between our two churches today. Hindsight always has 20/20 vision, and if we could live this story over, we would surely solve the problems faster and better. But living through it has helped us, the pastors, as well as many in our congregations, to grow, to define our ministries and to understand in a deeper way that each body of believers must work out its own salvation in fear and trembling.

So we ask, as you read, that you think deeply of the real issues, trying to avoid assigning tags such as "good guys" and "bad guys" to the personalities involved. Learn from the experiences of these church people that Christ can work even in the midst of conflict and misunderstanding to accomplish His purposes. The purpose of this book is to glorify God, not to justify men. We pray that it will be accomplished.

DR. WILLIAM LESLIE   DR. WARREN WIERSBE
LaSalle Street Church   *Moody Memorial Church*

Terror in the Afternoon

1

Terror in the Afternoon

STEVE UJVAROSY SAW the vacant-eyed young men lounging around the church steps and thought nothing of it. Maybe they were waiting to see Chuck Hogren, the young attorney who ran the church's Legal Aid Clinic. Steve, an engineer, was in a hurry to deposit the morning offering—almost $2,000; unusually good for a midsummer Sunday—and get home to dinner in Evanston. The sooner the better, for he didn't want to join the growing company of the mugged among the membership. You could get robbed and beaten up in broad day-light in Chicago's 18th Police District, which was renowned for high crime and police graft. Twenty-four of Mayor Daley's "finest," including the district commander, had only recently been indicted for extortion of neighborhood tavern owners.

Jake, the paunchy panhandler, saw the loungers, too, and hurried on. One of the most faithful attenders, he had mooched a couple of bucks from newcomers "to buy medicine for my poor, old sick mother." Now he was smacking his lips in anticipation of the booze he would buy with the morning's solicitations.

Others kept coming out through the squeaky, scarred doors of the imposing old church that had been built on LaSalle Street in 1882 and was soon to be named one of the 80 architectural "landmarks" in Chicago. Among the crowd were secretaries, students, teachers, so-

13

cial workers, young lawyers and doctors, tottering old people, a pair of giggling junior highs, and a couple with a freckle-faced first-grader begging to go to the beach.

They were bound for a variety of destinations: ethnic restaurants; a picnic in Lincoln Park; beehive, high rises that studded the lakefront; two-flats and four-flats further back in the city; dismal public housing; flea-trap street hotels; and, for a few families, homes in the suburbs. LaSalle people were always late leaving. Except for those in cell groups scattered around the city, most wouldn't see one another until the next Sunday.

The three loungers waited until the buzz of conversation ceased from inside. Then they moved around to the Elm Street side of the church where they would not be noticed by passing police cars. "Hey, we're in luck," one chortled when he noticed the side door was open and tied back with a clothes hanger for ventilation. Motioning to his companions to wait outside, he slipped catlike through the door.

Their prey was still inside. William Houghton Leslie, the broad-shouldered young pastor, had stayed around to lock up. His wife, Adrienne, and their four children were vacationing in Canada. He had taken them there and returned to work on his doctoral dissertation. In a couple of weeks he planned to go back to the wilderness for a few days of rest before driving the family home.

The church had a hired custodian, a student from the Moody Bible Institute, just three blocks down on LaSalle Street. But on Sundays, the staff took turns straightening up and locking the doors. Today, July 21, 1974, was the senior pastor's day.

"Bill," as everybody called him, was in no hurry to go home to an empty house. He puttered around in the tiny church office putting away a cassette recorder, locking a file cabinet, making notes on staff assignments for the coming week. The routine eased his tiredness as he reflected on the morning. He had preached on Esther—the third sermon in a series on Old Testament women. Several young career women in the church had commended him, remarking how much his consciousness had been raised on feminism.

The Sunday before, he had talked about Ruth's leaving her home-

14

land and going to a foreign country; "a daring thing for a single woman to do back then," he said. "Ruth showed us that faith does not settle down; faith takes a risk, gambles your life for God. You don't know how it's going to come out.

"Esther took that risk. She could have been killed for going to the king and asking that her people be spared. But instead of playing it safe she followed faith's call."

Usually there was a special speaker or panel for the Fellowship Hour that followed the 10:00 a.m. worship service. Today Bill had given a report of "the Lord's goodness to our church, that only ten years ago looked as if it might go down the drain."

There were a number of new Christians, he noted, including a black university professor, a girl who had been hospitalized for mental depression, a courier from the Satanist Process Church, a young woman who had burned two boxes of witchcraft books, and an artist who had opened her life to Christ as a result of contacts through a nearby Christian bookstore. A baptismal service would be held later in the summer at the lake.

The cell groups were flourishing. A foundation had just made a $5,000 grant to the Legal Aid Clinic. The Counseling Center had a waiting list. The ministry to senior citizens was growing. The day camp for neighborhood children was having exciting results. Two new interns had just come on the staff.

"Some of us old-timers can remember not too far back when many Evangelicals were saying we had departed from the faith and had become liberal. A few even suggested we were communist sympathizers. Now the same people who were condemning us are beginning to say, 'Hey, maybe this church can teach us something about ministering to the inner city.'

"We're being touted as a success symbol, a model for other churches, by some Evangelicals. I hope this won't go to our heads, for we're a long way from what we should be. But people are paying attention to us. Some of you met Senator Mark Hatfield when he was here a few months ago to look at our operations. I've been invited to Los Angeles to consult on a TV series called 'The Pastors.' A few years ago I was having speaking engagements canceled; now more calls are coming in than I can fulfill.

"But we mustn't get overconfident or think we have arrived. The big battles may still be ahead of us. The cost of discipleship will never be easy. Some of us right in this room may be called upon to risk our lives in faith ventures."

The wail of a siren broke into Bill's reflections as he closed the office and walked across the quiet vestibule and down the short hall on the Elm Street side. He saw that the side door was still open. Stepping outside to unwire the coat hanger, he noticed the two unfamiliar blacks sitting on the steps. He said hello, commented on the heat, and asked how they were doing. All the time he was thinking, "There's a third one inside." It was an old game that neighborhood youths had played many times. One would hide in the church while the doors were being locked. Then after the last staff person left, he would open the doors and let his friends inside. Sometimes it was to steal, more often it was just a lark. But it had never been funny to come back and find a hundred kids tearing through the building.

Locking the side door, Bill went around to all the favorite hiding places: the rest rooms, the subbasement, anywhere a person could conceal himself. Finding no one there, he started a final walk-through.

He saw the two fellows who had been outside as he came up the middle stairway toward the front vestibule. One held two clubs the size of bowling pins. Their companion had sprung from some unknown hiding place and let them in. Instinctively, Bill sensed what would happen next.

Without a word, the one with the clubs hit him on the head. As he rocked from the blow, the other one kicked him in the stomach. Then the one who had been hiding, whom he hadn't yet seen, struck him from behind.

Bill had been a three-sport athlete in high school and could have played varsity sports in college. He was still in good shape for a 42-year-old preacher. And he was one of a few whites who could walk unarmed in reasonable safety around the now all-black Cabrini-Green

Housing Project four blocks behind the church. Police had brought to Cabrini-Green a special foot patrol of 55 officers to reinforce the squad cars after snipers had killed two officers in 1970. Bill Leslie could walk alone because he was pastor of the one mostly white church that had stayed through the savage riots of the late '60s and had tried to help neighborhood people at hurting points.

Today he was a loser. He was one against three, and had he been a match for them, he would not have purposely injured an attacker. Furthermore, they apparently were from outside the neighborhood and didn't know him. He guessed they had just happened by, seen the people coming out, and thought of it as just another honky church—an easy mark for robbery.

They pounded him to the floor and tied his wrists, then kicked him around like a soccer ball while he rolled to protect his vital parts. His head roared with pain, and his stomach and legs twitched in torment. He thought of artist sketches of criminals in newspapers and kept trying to get a clear look at their faces. A pair of glazed eyes told him one was a drug addict. Then he remembered that assault victims were frequently killed for fear they would later identify their attackers.

"Give us the offering," one demanded.

"I don't have it," Bill gasped. "The treasurer took it to the bank."

"You're lyin'! Where's the bread?"

"I don't have it. In our church the preacher doesn't keep it."

Bill was on his back now, trying to protect his face. Suddenly the one wearing boots leaped onto his stomach and began jumping up and down all the way to his groin. At the same time another put his shoe on Bill's neck, grinding his heel against Bill's throat. Bill somehow managed to roll over again, causing the one on his stomach to fall against the wall. Angry, he grabbed a fire extinguisher and turned it on Bill. Fortunately, some children had almost emptied it a few weeks before—the first time this had happened—and it had not been refilled.

The one who had been on his neck had been knocked off balance also. Now he stood menacingly over Bill. "Rev, we know the preacher keeps the money. Tell us where it is or we'll give you some more."

17

"The treasurer took it to the bank," Bill protested again. "You can have all I've got. Take it."

They went through his pockets and found about $15.

"Watch him," the one who had done most of the talking told the others. "I'll look around."

Bill lay still for a few merciful minutes, praying, asking God for guidance. He remembered a story he had read of Turkish soldiers beating up an Armenian Christian. "What can your Jesus do for you now?" the soldiers had asked. "My Jesus can let me forgive you" was the reply.

The searcher came back shaking his head and looking very angry.

Bill, who had remained face down, spoke quickly. "I just want you to know that even though you're doing this to me, the Lord is present in my life, and He will allow me to forgive you."

"Shuddup! We don't need to hear that crap. Tie 'im up."

One of the two that had been guarding Bill went into the office and rummaged around. He came back with a day-camp T-shirt which he used for a gag. Another pulled Bill's pants down around his feet and tied his ankles with his belt.

The one who had looked for the money and who seemed to be the leader spoke softly, almost apologetically. "Rev, we've done so much of this, we know where we's goin'. But once when we were kids, we reached out for help and nobody would do nothin'. That's why we gotta do what we's doin'."

"Aw, cut out the jive talk, and let's blow him away."

"Naw, let's stuff him in the janitor's closet there. I ain't for killin' no preach."

Bill's head throbbed, his temples were bleeding, his neck was so swollen he could hardly swallow, and his lower body ached as if it had been put through a meat grinder. But he lay quietly while they debated his fate. He couldn't tell whether the threats of death were real or psychological coercion to make him tell where the money was hidden.

For himself, he wasn't afraid to die. Working in a neighborhood where life was cheap, he had long before come to terms with death. A Methodist pastor and his wife had been slashed to death nearby;

another Christian worker had been shoved against a viaduct wall and had his skull crushed. Why should he be any different? Hadn't he told the people only an hour before, "The cost of discipleship will never be easy"? Hadn't he pointed to Esther's venture of faith in risking her life for the Jews? Hadn't he frequently preached that God sometimes chooses to accomplish more through a person's death than his life?

"I say, let's blow him away. He'll pull us out of a lineup someday."

"You're crazy. I don't want no preach's blood on my hands."

Bill mentally braced himself for a shot or a new round of blows, hoping that if they did decide to kill him it wouldn't be too painful. He felt sad for Adrienne and the kids.

"Finish that ol' dis-ser-ta-shun and hurry back," little Scott had implored when he left them. Laurel, the oldest, had simply looked at him with her soft blue eyes and said nothing.

Now they might have to come for a funeral. If he had to die, why couldn't it have been after vacation, after the family had had a little more time to be together?

"C'mon, let's do it," he heard a voice snap impatiently.

Do what? Leave me dead . . . or alive? Bill Leslie—ex-college student body president, ex-pastor of the largest church of his denomination in Illinois at age 24, and ex-success at practically everything he had attempted before coming to this neighborhood— closed his eyes and waited for the verdict.

Winds of Change in the Windy City

2

Winds of Change in the Windy City

BEFORE THE TRAUMATIC '60s, blacks lounging on the church steps would have aroused suspicion. Someone would have questioned them and, if they had refused to move on, might even have called the police. The church at the corner of Elm and LaSalle was then for whites only.

As late as 1961 uninformed "coloreds" were being told they would feel more at home four blocks away at the Clybourn Gospel Mission. No matter that from their back porches they could hear the choir rehearsing. They might as well have lived in Mississippi. It was understood that the black turf stopped in the middle of the block halfway between the parallel streets of LaSalle and Wells. Civil rights lawyers called the northern practice "de facto segregation."

The two streets run from the towering canyons of the downtown Loop a mile away and end another mile further north near North Clark. LaSalle and Clark form a blunt arrow on which sits the historic Moody Memorial Church. A block beyond, Wells merges into Lincoln Avenue near the site of the old garage where six gangsters and one ordinary citizen were gunned down in a syndicate war on Valentine's Day, 1929.

LaSalle and Wells were among the 13 streets named on the original plot of Chicago, drawn in 1830 when the frontier prairie town beside Lake Michigan had less than a thousand inhabitants.

As part of the religious history of Chicago, the changes in the colorful near-north neighborhood form an essential backdrop for understanding how LaSalle Church became such a focal point for conflict in the 1960s.

After 1830, Chicago's population increased rapidly by immigration. The newcomers settled in ethnic sectors that made up a miniature patchwork of Old Europe: Germans, Scandinavians, Irish, Jews, Italians, Swedes, Poles, Czechs, Lithuanians, Croats, Greeks, and others. They built their own churches, baked their own bread, and elected their own aldermen to the City Council.

A colony of hardworking but unskilled Germans settled on the near-north side, just west of the "Gold Coast" mansions that lined the lakefront. They became the street cleaners, maids, and butlers for their elite neighbors.

As an ethnic sector moved up economically in Chicago, it moved out geographically from the core city, selling or renting shops and residences to the next wave of newcomers. It was so with the Germans and the Swedes that followed them. They prospered and began trickling north. Behind them came a flotsam of poorer ethnic groups. Neighborhood crime and vice increased until the term "Little Hell" came to describe the community.

This shift was in motion when a bearded young Yankee shoe salesman rented a market hall on Wells Street for a Sunday school. "Crazy" Moody, as he was dubbed by establishment churchgoers, rode a "missionary horse" around the neighborhood, handing out candy to street urchins who promised to help clean up a meeting hall.

Moody's Sunday school spiraled to 1,500—mostly people who were not sought by regular churches. Soon the school attracted nationwide attention. Newly elected President Abraham Lincoln, who had been nominated for the presidency only a few blocks away, came to observe, and was coaxed by Moody into giving the only speech he was ever known to present before a church group. Six years later the Sunday school became the Illinois Street Independent Church and installed a pastor. (Moody himself was never ordained and spent the rest of his life as an evangelist, becoming one of the most influential

24

American religious figures of the 19th century.) A Bible institute where students "learned by doing" also resulted. Then, after Moody's death in 1899, both the church and institute were renamed in his honor.

The Swedes had built the English Lutheran Church at the corner of LaSalle and Elm in 1882. It was a duplicate of hundreds of churches still standing in Europe since Reformation days. From the foundation to the two high turrets (one was later destroyed by lightning), every opening curved at the top to form a symbol of a worshiper reaching up to God with praying hands. A magnificent Good Shepherd stained glass window, tooled by Old World artistry, vaulted above massive twin doors. The lofty sanctuary ceiling was supported by oaklike metal trusses curving high above box pews. The opening to the minister's study also reached upward in a majestic sweep. Even the basement, with utility rooms, a kitchen, and a 40' x 50' square social hall, had Biblical scenes on stained glass windows all around.

About this time American Protestants began dividing over theology and social work. Despite Moody's social concern, his main financial support had come from big businessmen who tended to see labor organizers and social activists as radicals and anarchists. They wanted Christian workers to stick to soul-saving; never mind 17-hour days that kept fathers from family duties, five-dollar-a-week wages that drove shop girls into prostitution, and stinking tenements that harbored rats and disease. When, for example, Charles F. Goss, pastor of the Moody congregation from 1885-90, ventured that Christians should become concerned about the plight of the shop girls, he was told to "stick to the Gospel."

By the 1920s the sides had hardened into "modernists" and "fundamentalists." The modernists generally preached the ethics of Christ and promoted the kingdom of welfare government. The fundamentalists (known for championing five fundamentals: the virgin birth, substitutionary atonement, Christ's physical resurrection, His personal Second Coming, and the infallibility of Scripture) stressed separation from the world, personal evangelism, and the inevitable decay of society, which they predicted would soon culminate in the

25

return of Christ. The fundamentalists created a new subculture of "separated" Christians who pledged to refrain from card playing, movies, smoking, drinking, and dancing.

Moody Church prospered and in 1925 built a grand Romanesque sanctuary that seated 4,000. The most famous names among the fundamentalists expounded Scripture, usually verse-by-verse, from the pulpit. A mile down LaSalle Street, Moody Bible Institute (MBI) provided eager student workers for a network of mission Sunday schools scattered across ethnic and racial enclaves in Chicago.

The Italian Mission, begun in 1910, was located near the mother church. It met in the old Lutheran edifice at Elm and LaSalle. The stately building had been sold by the Swedish Lutherans to the Northside Holiness Church, who in turn sold the property in 1936 to Moody Church for $22,000, of which $15,000 was given by an Italian doctor/lay teacher. Four blocks further west, housed in a storefront, was the Clybourn Gospel Mission for blacks. Moody strategists felt people were more apt to affiliate with their own ethnic, racial, and economic groups.

By the end of World War II the Italians were departing the vicinity. Japanese Americans, newly released from Western concentration camps, quickly filled the row houses and apartments. Elm-LaSalle Bible Church, as it was now called (though still a mission of Moody Church), took on an Oriental flavor—briefly. Possessing more job skills than their predecessors, the Japanese began leaving in the early '50s, making way for poor Appalachian whites and Puerto Ricans.

Over the years the one stable group in Elm-LaSalle Church had been the blue-collar MBI employees. (MBI faculty living in the area tended to prefer Moody Church.) The MBI lay leaders quickly adapted to the influx of the new ethnic groups, tailoring Sunday morning services to the Southerners and providing an afternoon Spanish-speaking Sunday school for the Puerto Ricans. Straying blacks continued to be told that the Clybourn Mission was for them. The building was crowded Sunday morning and afternoon. With MBI students teaching classes and also leading weekday Bible clubs, scores of children made professions of faith.

The mother church hadn't been doing too well since the resignation of the renowned H. A. Ironside in 1948. Crowds of 4,000 coming from a radius of 100 miles had dwindled to less than 1,500. Still, many felt that the personable Alan Redpath was every bit as good a preacher, though some considered him a bit too frank in his applications to life. Redpath, like his predecessors, traveled a lot, speaking at Bible conferences for other churches. One trip in February, 1959, took him to the First Baptist Church of Pekin in downstate Illinois. He was amazed at how much the church had grown in three years. With over a thousand members, it had become the largest Conservative Baptist church in the state. And the pastor, Bill Leslie, was only 27 years old.

"This is phenomenal," Redpath commented to Bill. "I hope you stay at least ten years."

"Well, we're thinking of leaving," Bill confessed. "When I came here three years ago from Wheaton College, all I lacked for my master's was my thesis. Adrienne has been sick a lot, and I've been so busy with the church I haven't had time to write it. But we've prayed and concluded that the first priority should be to finish my education. Prexy [President V. Raymond Edman of Wheaton] once told me, 'The bigger the foundation, the larger the building.'

"Lately I've been studying the social change that resulted from the Wesleyan revivals in England. I understand Garrett, the Methodist seminary in Evanston, has a good program on Wesley and the social aspects of the Gospel. The courses are tied in with a Ph.D. program at Northwestern University. After Wheaton, I might go for that."

Redpath quickly switched gears. "I've been asking God for a youth pastor. Would you consider it? You could go to school at the same time."

It seemed providential—working at the famous Moody Church under Redpath, while attending graduate school. "Yes," Bill said enthusiastically, with Adrienne's concurrence.

Redpath flew home the next day and was back with an offer before nightfall. Bill resigned the church (his first pastorate), and he and Adrienne moved in May into a new house in Wheaton in time for the arrival of their first child, Laurel.

27

Wheaton was 30 miles from Moody Church, but the Leslies felt Adrienne and the baby would be better off in a suburb than in an apartment downtown. Also Garrett-Northwestern professors advised Bill that a three-year Bachelor of Divinity degree from the Wheaton College Graduate School would be a better prerequisite to their doctoral program than an M.A. This was acceptable to Redpath and the Moody Church board as long as Bill gave at least 40 hours a week to church ministries.

Bill came to Moody with a gilt-edged fundamentalist dossier. He had been a leader in high school, church, and Youth for Christ in Milan, Ohio. His grandfather had been a pioneer missionary to Africa and, as a result of taking Teddy Roosevelt on safaris, had stayed at the White House while on furloughs.

Bill's father, William Houghton, had been a coach at the high school where Bill was captain of the basketball team for three years and had also lettered in baseball. Despite his physical prowess, Bill opted to major in music—he played eight different instruments. While at fundamentalist Bob Jones University he operated the night switchboard for 30¢ an hour and managed to become a big man on campus. After his freshman year he joined a summer Gospel team going to Europe. The next summer he went to Latin America. His third year he was elected president of the student body.

That year, 1953, a faculty rebellion erupted against the school's ruling family. Asked to sign a loyalty oath to the administration, Bill declined, saying that while he supported the "general purposes" of the school, he "could not in good conscience" approve all that went on. President Bob Jones, Sr., immediately ordered him to leave. He was not even allowed to tell his friends good-bye. The following fall he transferred to Wheaton College where he completed his undergraduate work. From Wheaton, Bill had gone to his first pastorate, in Pekin.

The youth program blossomed at Moody Church under Bill Leslie. Everybody seemed to like him. He was the fundamentalists' ideal of what a young preacher should be: blond, blue-eyed, broad-shouldered, conservative in theology and politics, and super-talented.

28

Adrienne Leslie, however, looked downright worldly to some of the members. The tall, stunning blond would have been a natural for the cover of *Vogue*. She wore stylish broad-brimmed hats, used eye shadow and lipstick, and even painted her fingernails. Her appearance caused some frowns among older constituents, but the girls cheered her on.

The youth departments grew, but the church that Moody founded continued losing families to suburban congregations. By 1960 attendance had dropped below 2,000—one Sunday night only 55 came to a service—and there was talk of following the trend among downtown churches and relocating in a more stable neighborhood.

The pastoral staff and some board members held long informal discussions about the viability of remaining close to the downtown area. Bill felt they should stay in the city and strive to become a neighborhood church. "I can see that in the old days there was need for a great church center," he said. "Moody Church had the best preachers and the only missionary conferences in the Chicago area. People drove in from Indiana and Wheaton and all over. Then the suburban churches started getting good preachers and began their own missionary programs. Now we need to gear up our staff and our mentality to reach the near-north side."

Bill was among the thinkers in the second generation of fundamentalists who felt churches had too much real estate which was being used inadequately. He noted that salaries of custodians at Moody Church totaled twice that of the three-member pastoral staff. He suggested the church tear down the hallowed sanctuary and build an apartment high rise. "Rental income can pay the mortgage," he argued, "and the church can use the lower two floors for worship, Bible study, youth activities, and community facilities."

While these and other ideas were being discussed, Redpath invited the religion writers of the four major Chicago newspapers to lunch at the North Park Hotel's restaurant. "We want to remain in the city," he told them, "but we'll need your help with some publicity."

"How many black members do you have?" one asked pointedly.

"Well, none yet," Redpath stuttered. "But we have a few adults

29

attending and a larger number of children in Sunday school.''

"Well, when you integrate the church membership, give us another call," the writer said.

"There are a few Negroes at the Institute," Bill noted after the reporters had left. "Some sing in the chorale. When the chorale came to Pekin a couple of deacons warned me of possible trouble. They said a lot of people were still boasting that no Negroes had ever stayed overnight in the town. Adrienne and I volunteered to keep the blacks. Nothing happened. The next year when the chorale came everybody wanted to have them. They had become a novelty.

"Bob Jones has a policy against enrolling blacks, but lets them work in the kitchen. Students complained to me that the blacks got the dirtiest and the heaviest work, and that anyone offering to help them was threatened with discipline. I was president of the student body and couldn't do anything. It made me so angry."

"It's a shame. A disgrace!" Redpath snorted. "It isn't the will of our Lord. Bill, we're going to do something." They decided Bill should propose to the membership committee of the church board that international students such as Africans and Indians be allowed to join as student members. With Redpath's strong urging, the motion passed. But Redpath and Bill were absent from the next meeting and it was rescinded.

Redpath refused to let the issue die. "It's hypocrisy to send missionaries abroad and not allow membership to internationals when they come here to study," he insisted. The committee recanted and agreed that African and Indian students could join the church after all.

Everything went well until Redpath came back with step two. "Two young Negroes whose family has been attending our church for years have applied for membership. Many of you know them. Marjorie Branch has an undergraduate degree from Wheaton College and a master's from the University of Chicago. She works for the city school system. Her brother, John, is an architectural student."

Board members argued back and forth whether the two should be accepted. Objectors said having "colored" members would certainly drive out of the church some people who didn't believe in integration.

Proponents said Moody Church should do what was right; the board should lead instead of follow the constituency. When it looked as if the battle was lost, Redpath put himself on the line. "If you vote this down, you will have my resignation," he declared. "I will not be a part of any fellowship that rejects some of God's people."

They voted to accept the Branches into membership, although in a way it seemed a hollow victory. Some refused to shake hands with the new members when they were received into the church.

Meanwhile, Elm-LaSalle, which was about halfway between Moody Church and MBI, continued to harvest the neighborhood's children. But though the numbers looked good, the branch church was financially weak and quite dependent upon Moody Church.

Seven or eight years before there had been more adults. Sunday school attendance had reached a high mark of 307. Pastor Larry Roland had asked the Moody Church board to purchase additional property for expansion. Turned down, he requested congregational independence. The board dampened this idea by maintaining that Elm-LaSalle couldn't survive financially on its own.

Attendance took a nosedive under Roland's successor. Then Redpath brought on Jim Johnson, a missionary returned from Africa, who had enrolled at MBI. By recruiting MBI students and bringing in a parade of speaking and singing personalities, Johnson brought the numbers back up.

Bill Leslie and Jim Johnson played basketball together at the neighborhood "Y" and became good friends. Johnson had become a Christian at Moody Church while studying journalism at Northwestern University. A foreign mission society then sent him to Africa to train a Nigerian national to take over the editorship of an evangelistic magazine. To his dismay, Johnson found the missionaries unwilling to let the publication go. Caught in the cross fire, he had returned home an emotional wreck. "Redpath sent me here," he told Bill. "Elm-LaSalle has been my salvation. I love the work. There's never a dull moment.

"You won't believe what happened the other day." Johnson laughed. "I was sitting in the office, beating the pigeons back through

31

a broken window, when two guys walked in wearing black coats and hats pulled down. 'We need you to read over a guy, Reverend.' 'What? Where?' I asked in puzzlement. 'Yeah, read over him up at the funeral home. Tomorrow afternoon. We'll pick you up at two.'

"They came in a long black car, drove over to North Avenue, and marched me through the empty chapel, to a plain pine box. I opened my Bible to give a little sermon. 'Reverend,' one said in a low, gruff voice, 'just read over him.' So I read a psalm. Then they marched me out, slipped me 20 bucks at the door, and said, 'That's it.' A couple of months later I read in the *Tribune* that this funeral home had been raided as a Mafia hangout. Then I realized the two guys were hoods. They must have bumped this fella off, then had a tinge of remorse and decided to give him a decent sendoff. I've never seen them since."

They talked a while longer, then Bill asked, "What do you plan to do when you finish at the Institute?"

"Well, you know I've pestered the Moody Church board for independence. I told them it's about time they turned loose this 24-year-old child. They kept saying, 'How are you going to make it without us?' I said, 'I can go to the mission field and build churches and come home and can't. It doesn't make sense.'

"But Redpath told me later that they were really afraid Elm-LaSalle might get into the wrong hands and go liberal.

"Perhaps it's just as well I don't hang around. Some of the people and I don't see eye to eye on the blacks. I say we should welcome them regardless of what happens. They think the blacks will drive off the Southerners and that we should keep sending them over to the Clybourn Mission. Nuts! Do you know what the blacks told me? 'We don't want no mission. We're no target for white missionaries.'

"And I don't blame them for feeling that way. I told Redpath the board should junk this mission idea and get on with building a church."

Bill smiled. "Are you going to fight it out?"

"I don't think so. The leading I have now is to do graduate work and serve the Lord in journalism. I've applied at Michigan State."

When Johnson left in the fall of '61, Redpath asked Bill if he would like to take Elm-LaSalle. "The pay will be the same, but you might have more future there," he counseled.

Bill was interested, so Redpath suggested the change to the Moody Church board. The church officers said they hated to lose Bill since he was doing such a good job with their young people but conceded his being at Elm-LaSalle would take a worry off their minds. "We know you're straight," one said to Bill approvingly.

Bill felt a couple of things should be made clear. "One, I'll need a desk and chair in the office." They smiled consent. "Two, I will expect you to give us independence and sell us the building." Hearing no dissent, he went on. "When I was at Pekin, we had a branch church that became independent. We had put a lot of money into their building, but we sold it to them for a token dollar. I think that's the norm elsewhere." Because still no one voiced objections, Bill concluded they were in agreement.

On September 8, 1961, he preached his first sermon as Elm-LaSalle's pastor before about 150 in a half-full sanctuary. It wasn't the first time he had stood on the worn gray carpeting behind the pulpit. He had preached before in Jim Johnson's absence. Now he was the leader.

He had a lot of ideas and plenty of self-confidence. He was sure he could do in Chicago what he had done in Pekin.

When the Bubble Burst

3

When the Bubble Burst

BILL EXUDED SELF-CONFIDENCE as he took over the pastorate of Elm-LaSalle. He had fond memories of his days in Pekin where he had preached and promoted in the style taught at Bob Jones and Wheaton. He had brought in entertaining special speakers: youth evangelists, Christian athletes, beauty queens, and successful business executives; all to show that "a Christian could go first class."

He had promoted Sunday school contests that whipped up a competitive spirit between classes and inspired evangelistic visitation, and directed missionary conferences that featured dramatic speakers along with flags, maps, and curios from around the world.

He had made some daring innovations like taking the young people skating, considered "dancing on wheels" by disapproving fundamentalists. The church had even gotten to the point of allowing missionary films in the church sanctuary on Sunday nights.

Bill presumed that similar programs would bring even greater successes in Chicago, so he began pushing the Pekin game plan in the big city.

But things weren't quite the same. In Pekin he had his new bride at his side helping with all his plans; now Adrienne was kept busy 30 miles away with two-year-old Laurel and newborn Lisa. Adrienne got into the city only on Sundays.

And a setback came in Bill's graduate work. The previous May he had completed his seminary program only to be told by an official at Garrett-Northwestern that the Wheaton studies were unaccredited. The man felt genuinely sorry for Bill and offered a concession. "You can take an M.A. here and we'll let 72 hours of that count on your Ph.D. Now hurry and get in your transcripts."

Bill immediately wrote Wheaton and Bob Jones. Wheaton replied at once but there was no response from the South Carolina school.

A second, third, and fourth request went unheeded. Bob Jones' only response was to cash Bill's $1 checks. Now it was too late to enroll for the fall semester.

He went back to Garrett-Northwestern and begged for understanding. "I can't budge them. They must not like either of us."

By this time his Bob Jones transcript had become a cause celebre among the Methodist professors. Finally the admitting dean snorted, "If they're that mad at you, you must be all right. We'll get you in the second semester. Just get us a copy of your Wheaton record."

The one good thing about the transcript imbroglio was that Bill had more time to work at Elm-LaSalle during his crucial first four months there. "We'll be having double worship services by Christmas," he confidently promised Adrienne.

But all his razzle-dazzle promotions couldn't counteract the forces at Elm-LaSalle that were beyond his control.

The Puerto Ricans had begun moving away before his arrival. The Spanish Sunday school was closed. Now the Appalachians to the east and north were departing.

The same scenario happened repeatedly. Someone would go to visit a family that had been in church the previous Sunday and find their apartment or house empty and the neighbors unaware of where they had gone. The realtor signs and construction projects all around told what was happening. The row houses and tenements were being replaced by luxury apartments, boutiques, novelty shops, restaurants, taverns, and the like. The politicians and entrepreneurs called the arty new development "Old Town." Conveniently close to downtown hotels, the development was expected to draw a mint of dollars from tourists and conventioneers.

Refusing to be discouraged, Bill went after the long-neglected blacks who lived to the west. Most were indifferent, some almost hostile. "I ain't goin' to that church," a mother of seven snapped. "We tried once and were sent away. If we weren't good 'nuff then, we ain't good 'nuff now." But Bill persisted and a few blacks started coming.

The area to the west wasn't all black, but it was getting that way fast. In the fall of 1961 many whites still lived in the giant new Cabrini-Green housing project for low-income families. Altogether, some 17,000 people were packed in the 15 multistory high rises and the 55 sections of modest row houses. Several MBI employee families who were active in Elm-LaSalle lived in Cabrini-Green, as well as in private housing around the neighborhood. But they were looking for safer places to live. Others caught in the Old Town development were searching for cheaper housing. The real estate bonanza in Old Town had caused some landlords to raise rent as much as $100 a month with no improvements. MBI employees simply couldn't afford that.

Fewer MBI students were attending. Bill knew why. Jim Johnson had been a student and was on the campus every day, while he seldom had time.

December came. Instead of realizing two services, Bill noted that attendance was half what it had been when he came.

It was not a season to be jolly. Bill felt deflated, crushed. He had pulled every trick out of his bag, bringing in the best speakers and musicians, awarding candy and other attendance prizes, giving a high-keyed sales pitch for visitation in practically every service. Multitudes lived all around the church, yet few seemed to care about coming.

The methods were tried and tested. There had to be only one answer. "Lord, show me my sin," he begged. When no moral infraction came to light, he felt worse. "The Spirit of the Lord has departed from me," he moaned. Still the pastor and the church survived. The snow melted and the first buds of spring came. Bill was finally enrolled in graduate school. He was also still determined to build a strong church.

Perhaps a retreat would boost discouraged spirits and inspire fresh commitments. He reserved the Moody Church camp near Antioch, Illinois, and invited an old Wheaton classmate to speak. Francis Steele was a former Inter-Varsity Christian Fellowship staffer and now Home Secretary for the North Africa Mission to Muslims.

To this long-time friend Bill poured out his discouragement. "I know just how you feel," Steele sympathized. "I felt the same way during my first missionary term among Muslims."

"Adrienne and I once thought of being missionaries," Bill interrupted. "We were interested in Taiwan. I'm not sure now I would have made it. I can't even carry out the Lord's commission in Chicago."

"What is His commission?" Steele asked rhetorically. "Go, make disciples, preach, teach. Have you noticed, Bill, that in the Greek text of Matthew 28 'make disciples' is the only imperative in the verse? That's our job. Not to win the multitudes, but to disciple those whom He entrusts to us, whether they be many or few."

A new light began to dawn. "Disciple means to teach, train, build up in the faith."

"Exactly, Bill. That's our main job."

A heavy load of guilt rolled away. No longer did Bill feel compelled to constantly be pressing people about salvation or church attendance. He did not have to build a big church. His responsibility was to preach God's Word with integrity and to disciple those whom God put under his pastoral care. After all, as Francis Steele also pointed out, Jesus spent most of His time with only 12 men.

Bill began paying more attention to the steady, loyal members of the church. One of the most faithful was Sunday school superintendent Dick Reid, a florist who also served as Elm-LaSalle's part-time youth director. Dick felt Elm-LaSalle had been too much of a children's mission in the past. "It's great for the Moody students. But we've got to reach staying people, or we'll never be strong enough to launch out on our own."

"I've been thinking this myself," Bill agreed. "Suburban churches are competing for the MBI students. When I come down from

Wheaton on Sunday mornings, I see the buses lined up at the curb. Jim Johnson told the administration that this doesn't make sense, that they should channel the students into inner-city churches. But I can't see us fighting for them. Lately, I've felt the urge to go after the students and young professionals in the medical, law, and nursing schools around town. Nobody is sending buses after them."

"Well, what are we waiting for?" Reid asked.

They started with a few students Bill already knew. One was Dr. Bud Hurst, a surgical resident at Wesley Hospital and a former Wheaton student body president.

Bill began praying and studying the Bible with Hurst. At an evening Bible discussion in Hurst's apartment, 47 medical students, interns, and residents turned up.

A few days later Hurst was preparing for an operation when his nurse, Joyce Klinger, asked, "Are you a Christian, doctor?" "Yes, I am," he replied. "How did you know? And why do you ask?"

"I saw you bow your head and pray before eating in the cafeteria. We did that in our home back in Canada. My parents were good Christians, but I threw it all over after coming to Chicago. My friends think I lead a pretty exciting life. I'm also a model. Actually, my life is terribly empty, and I haven't found anything worthwhile to live for."

Later Hurst explained to her how he had found purpose through a personal relationship with Jesus Christ. Then he brought her to Elm-LaSalle. She became a Christian and grew rapidly in the faith. Two years later she returned to Canada as a staff member for Campus Crusade for Christ.

Chuck Hogren, a soft-spoken young lawyer, was a different story. One day he simply dropped by the church to see how Bill was getting along. A couple of years before he had participated in a few discussions when Bill was at Moody Church and he was a student at the Northwestern Law School.

Bill shared some of the struggles of Elm-LaSalle, then asked, "How are you liking law practice?"

"Oh, fine, fine," Chuck replied. "I'm in probate and handling estates. I'm living with my folks in West Chicago [a far western suburb] and still attending the Bible Church there.''

Chuck had been an undergraduate at Wheaton with Bill. But they hadn't really known each other. It was time to get better acquainted.

''I grew up in a Mission Covenant Church on the south side,'' Chuck recalled. ''Our family moved to the suburbs just before the first blacks moved in. It was a foregone conclusion that I would go to Wheaton College.

''While at Wheaton I was a volunteer for the inner-city program. We rounded up kids for mission Sunday schools. Visiting in their homes was an eye-opener. I remember once going into an old tenement hotel where the smell was so bad I could hardly stand it. At the head of four flights of rickety stairs, I found a mother and two or three ragged children living in a single dark room with no windows. It really shook me. I hadn't known people lived like that in Chicago.''

''From what I've seen, that isn't unusual around here,'' Bill commented.

''Is there something I can do?'' Chuck suddenly offered. ''Perhaps help out in the Sunday school?''

''I was hoping you'd ask that,'' Bill laughed. ''Right now we're missing a junior teacher. I just happen to have the teaching materials right in my desk.''

''I'll try,'' Chuck pledged.

Bill didn't see much of Chuck the next few weeks. With graduate study, commuting back and forth to his home in Wheaton, and church work, Bill had practically no spare time. Then Chuck showed up in Bill's office again, frowning. He tossed some Sunday school workbooks on the desk.

''The kids giving you a hard time?'' Bill asked.

''Oh, it isn't that. We get along fine. But some of them can't read. They can't do the work. I don't understand how they get promoted in school.''

''That's what I've been hearing from other teachers,'' Bill said. ''What do you think can be done?''

Maybe we could tutor them. I've heard that Fourth Presbyterian over on Michigan Avenue has been doing it.''

42

Bill smiled encouragement. "Why don't you check into it, Chuck? Maybe our young adults could take it on as a project."

Chuck asked Jerry Hazelrigg, the pastoral assistant who was in charge of the tutoring at Fourth Presbyterian, to come and talk with Elm-LaSalle's young adults. Acting on a newspaper story, he also wrote for help to a graduate student who had a tutoring program at the University of Chicago.

The two outsiders inspired Elm-LaSalle's young adults to believe they could do something. They bought about $50 of educational materials and started tutoring on Sunday afternoons. About 20 youngsters, mostly black, came for one-on-one assistance.

Then, much to Bill and Chuck's surprise, some of the older members objected. "I can see where using the Gospel of John and Bible stories would be all right," one person said. "But you're using secular materials that have no place in the church." This member served on Elm-LaSalle's board, which the Moody Church board had placed in charge of most of the branch church's business. He felt that the young adults had been presumptuous in going ahead with the tutoring on their own.

"It's just an experiment," Bill explained. "When we see how it's working, we'll get approval from the board." The complainer seemed satisfied. And Bill was not worried as long as Redpath was at Moody Church. He felt Redpath would be sympathetic toward the tutoring project.

Meanwhile, Bill had been studying at Garrett the writings of Calvin, Luther, and Wesley on the Sermon on the Mount. The views of the Reformers contrasted with what he had been taught at Bob Jones.

The Presbyterian, Lutheran, and Methodist founders had applied the hard teachings of Jesus directly to daily life. Wesley saw the Kingdom of God as both present and future. Believers were already in the Kingdom, he said, and should practice the Kingdom truths presented by Jesus in the Gospels. Fundamentalist dispensationalists tended to take their cues for daily living "under grace" from the Epistles, drawing only moral analogies from the teachings of Jesus.

The teachings of Wesley and other Reformers led Bill to make a

43

major shift in his preaching. He began talking about the Kingdom in the present tense. Christians should be "salt" and "light" in society and try to help people in the here and now. Not that society was perfectable. Only the redemption of individuals into a kingdom ruled by Christ could bring in a new eternal order. But Christ was to be the example, with His disciples following in His steps.

The dispensationalists at Elm-LaSalle became puzzled. Their new pastor's preaching was running in unfamiliar patterns. Some were bothered by his applications. Loving your neighbors, Bill said, called for helping them at points of felt need. If illiterate, teach them to read and write. If out of work, help them find jobs. If sick, see that they get medical care. The dispensationalists could hardly quarrel with doing this individually. But Bill was calling for the church to become corporately involved in such human services, and he pointed to the Sunday afternoon tutoring as a start—not as bait to draw persons under the "sound of the Gospel" but as a means of aiding suffering human beings.

Jesus opened Himself to the outcasts of first-century Jewish society, Bill also noted. He mingled with Samaritans, tax collectors, lepers, even prostitutes, and others whom the religious establishment avoided. If Elm-LaSalle was to follow Jesus, all ministries of the church should be totally available to all people.

Bill was also being influenced by Inter-Varsity Christian Fellowship. Because the IVCF national headquarters was just around the corner on Astor Street, he found it convenient to wander over for coffee breaks. IVCF was then discovering in Scripture what Bill had been learning from Wesley and other Evangelical reformers. They called it the doctrine of the whole person.

Most IVCF chapters were on state and private college campuses. The staff members, who had come up through the student groups, had been more exposed to new currents of thought than had graduates of fundamentalist schools. They were aware of the holistic trends in the healing sciences toward treating patients as physical, mental, social, and spiritual persons. The Inter-Varsity people felt it was time Evangelicals did this, too. To preach salvation from sin and acceptance of grace was crucial and essential. But redemption from other bonds should be offered also.

IVCF worked closely with the Nurses Christian Fellowship and the Christian Medical Society. Local NCF and CMS leaders encouraged nurses and medical students to attend the discussions Bill had started.

By 1963 Elm-LaSalle membership was shifting toward graduate students and young professionals dissatisfied with the old forms of fundamentalism. These second-generation fundamentalists preferred being called "Evangelicals." They were part of a rising tide, inspired in varying degrees by the new Fuller Seminary, Billy Graham, *Christianity Today*, Wheaton College, and others whom many fundamentalists felt had moved away from the old foundations. Harold Ockenga, the first president of Fuller Seminary and also pastor of Boston's Park Street Church, claimed fundamentalists had abdicated "leadership and responsibility in the societal realm." The "New Evangelicals" (Ockenga's term) would bring "a social philosophy" to personal salvation, he predicted.

Surprisingly, the chief agitator for faster change at Elm-LaSalle was not one of the IVCF staffers or young doctors, but an MBI student, Gene Brack, the church's music director. Brack shocked the elders by coming to prayer meeting and leading hymns without a tie. Just when they were getting over this, he began chiding the church board about its slowness in overcoming a mentality of racism.

Racial change and rising rents had already made the MBI employees restive. Bill's practical applications of the Gospel and the highly educated newcomers made them feel even less comfortable. Brack was now adding fuel to the fire.

At the same time the young adults were pressing for representation on the Elm-LaSalle board. Bill presented their case to the chairman, who agreed they should have a voice. One of the first newcomers to be elected was Chuck Hogren.

The board additions were made just before the controversial tutoring program came up for a vote. The conservatives repeated their objections: "The church building is not the place for secular education. If we are going to teach kids to read, we should use the Bible. If we can't use the Bible, let's stay out of social things."

Speaking in his usually quiet, deliberate manner, Chuck Hogren took a stand for tutoring. "We would prefer that the schools do this," he said. "But they don't have the personnel to give kids who are behind individual attention. They just keep promoting them through high school and graduate them as functional illiterates. Since the schools can't help and the kids don't have help at home, I see nothing unchristian about allowing volunteers to help them at church."

The arguments pro and con continued. Finally, Bill spoke up: "All of you know John and Joy Anderson who are missionaries from our church and serving with the Wycliffe Bible Translators. They've just finished translating the Gospel of Mark into an American Indian dialect. Now they're teaching members of the tribe to read. They're using the same educational materials which we have here. We pray for them every week. Some of us send them financial support. Does it make sense for us to support them in doing something that we refuse to do here?"

The new board members saved the tutoring program, for it passed by only one vote.

Afterward came the usual handshakes and affirmations to "pull together." But it was obvious that some of the spirit had gone out of the losing side. Tutoring with secular educational materials had become to them a troublesome symbol of what the church could become.

Then, to make the situation more difficult, Alan Redpath resigned from Moody Church to accept the pulpit of the famed Charlotte Chapel in Edinburgh, Scotland. Redpath's leaving was a great disappointment to Bill and the "New Evangelicals" at Elm-LaSalle. But some Chicago fundamentalists were glad to see him go. The fiery Englishman had preached on the Sermon on the Mount during MBI's annual Founder's Week. He charged some dispensationalists with scissoring out more Bible passages than liberals, though for different reasons.

Bill and Redpath had been close. Redpath understood Bill's tight schedule and had not insisted he attend all the biweekly board meetings and weekly staff meetings at Moody Church. Instead, they got together over coffee and discussed the happenings at Elm-LaSalle.

Now Elm-LaSalle's vital link with the Moody Church board was gone. Without Redpath to smooth the way, Bill worried that the board might not understand all the little branch church was doing.

Stormy Weather

4

Stormy Weather

THE "UNDERSTANDING" BILL HAD with Moody Church began dissipating after Redpath left. Now instead of reporting informally to the senior minister every week or so, Bill was expected to attend all official meetings. This meant that besides three congregational services each week, Bill had the Elm-LaSalle monthly board meeting, the weekly Moody Church board meeting, and the Tuesday afternoon staff meeting at the parent church. The most important meeting came with the Moody Church trustee committee, which was responsible to the full board for Elm-LaSalle's affairs. This committee met before the regular board meeting and invariably had difficulty finishing its business. Since Elm-LaSalle was always last on the agenda, Bill frequently had to sit through the deliberations for nothing. With his tight schedule, it seemed a galling waste of time.

Each of the three major compartments in Bill's life kept begging for more attention. There was his family in Wheaton, which he left at 5:30 a.m. on weekdays and did not see again until around 11:00 p.m. The girls were asleep at those times and he could only look in on them. There were classes at Garrett-Northwestern in the mornings and library research throughout the day. There was church work in the evenings—counseling, sermon preparation, organizational meetings, youth programs. Adrienne kept reminding him that he was becoming a

51

stranger to her. His professors kept suggesting that if he intended to be a scholar he should spend more time with the books. And board members at Moody Church kept saying, "Where were you, Bill? We missed you last week."

The small-group movement was now flowing through lay channels in Protestant denominations and was seeping into fundamentalist ranks. The young disenchanted Evangelicals at Elm-LaSalle were eyeing the movement with interest.

Sunday school, they said, was only one of the traditional church structures that were not meeting their needs. The worship service was a performance by the preacher, choir, and soloist; prayer meeting (then called "The Hour of Power") a boring pretense where people intoned tired generalities and cliches; Sunday school a verse-by-verse Bible drag-a-long where the stark issues of daily living were hardly touched and where diverse opinions were seldom voiced; church life in general a meeting of Christians on superficial levels. "We don't feel close because we don't know one another," the young people protested to Bill. "We can't help one another because we can't express our deeply felt needs."

Bill had reached the same conclusions himself. He felt fundamentalists were making poor grades in building personal relationships on four counts:

First, their Bible study was dry and abstract, with little application to hurting areas of life.

Second, they stressed human depravity and unworthiness so much that this led to loss of self-esteem. He winced inwardly every time he heard the hymn phrase "for such a worm as I." How could you love your neighbor as yourself if you didn't love yourself?

Third, they had little deep fellowship. Conversation at church suppers seldom went beyond discussing family, business, hobbies, sermons, and missionaries. He had known church "pillars" who could quote Bible verses by the chapter yet were not really close to anybody.

Fourth, they made little provision for interaction and exercise of spiritual gifts within the local body of believers. The teacher or preacher was central with individuals relating to him, not to one another. Bill realized his own approach in past years had been much like other fundamentalist pastors: "You (the congregation) sit still while I instill." The pastor was to do the work of the ministry; the laity were to pay and pray; perhaps teach Sunday school; witness verbally about sin, the Savior, and salvation; and serve on church housekeeping committees.

A recovery of the sort of relationships experienced by Christians in other centuries seemed overdue.

Having already learned from John Wesley's sermons, Bill was now intrigued by his methods (from which came the name "Methodists," meaning "after a way"). Bill agreed with some church historians that it had not been Wesley's preaching that had saved England from bloody revolution. It had been his "way" of organizing converts into a network of small, supportive "societies," under the supervision of lay preachers. There was a lay leader for each circuit of societies and a treasurer in each group who collected money and dispersed funds to members in need. In times of terrible injustice and high unemployment, the believers had given spiritual, social, and economic support to one another.

Hadn't the first Christians experienced such supportive relationships? They had worshiped in house churches and rented halls before the Emperor Constantine declared Christianity a legal religion in the fourth century. Persecution and poverty made them interdependent and mutually supportive. The love they expressed for one another attracted outsiders starved for intimacy and companionship, just as Jesus had predicted: "By this all men will know that you are my disciples, if you have love for one another."

Bill was convinced that Elm-LaSalle needed to move in this direction, but he wasn't sure where to start. Acting too hastily and without adequate support could split the church and bring the censure of the Moody Church board. Bill decided to go slow and do nothing presumptuously.

He felt it the better part of valor not to alter the old but to let the new run alongside it in anticipation that the best would prevail. So he announced that small Bible study groups would meet on Sunday afternoon at the church and talk about whatever they wished. Lack of transportation and the danger of being on the streets at night made week night meetings impractical. There were only two cars in the congregation, the Leslies' and one other.

The groups turned out to be more of a burden than a blessing. Chuck Hogren, for example, had Sunday school, morning worship, tutoring, cell groups, young adult fellowship, and evening service—all on his day of rest. But the younger members were determined to have "cells."

A cell started with an awkward reading around of a Bible passage, followed by a few questions and comments little different from what was heard in Sunday school, then quickly slid into a me-and-my-problems moan-fest. To the extent, however, that some honest confessions were made and sympathy and prayer offered, the groups were helpful. Some of the people, for example, admitted they had only been roleplaying a life-style they hated.

As Henrietta, a trim brunette nursing student from California stated, "When I lost interest in YFC [Youth for Christ], my parents sent me to a Bible college. For awhile I played holy. I bit my tongue whenever I felt angry. I tried to be as plain as possible. No lipstick or nail polish. I wore my hair in braids. And it helped that I had freckles. Finally I realized I couldn't drip sweetness from every pore. This wasn't me. So I rebelled and ended up being confined to the dorm the whole last semester. I was in trouble all the time. Oh, once my housemother offered to let me go to YFC rallies with a fish-eyed guy she had picked out for me. He was 'God's will' for my life, she said. As much as I wanted to get out of the dorm, I couldn't stand him.

"After graduating, I was hired as a counselor at a Bible camp. They had the 'six-inch' rule. The opposite sex couldn't sit touching one another on a couch; boys and girls couldn't swim together. Every night we got a hellfire and brimstone sermon that scared kids down the aisles. If you were sensitive at all, they could always stir up some guilt. I couldn't counsel anybody. I was strapped with guilt the whole three months I was there.

"It wasn't my parents—they were real people—but the system that had been fostered on me. I kept thinking I'd get over it, but I guess that all my life I'll be digging out fundamentalist rot."

A few others were even more bitter about what they considered a false set of values imposed on them. "You mustn't dance. You mustn't go to the picture show. You mustn't do this or that," a law student parroted his parents. "It was worse at church. We were to be separated and holy witnesses. Bull! If I ever won anybody to that kind of thing, I didn't win them to Christianity.

"What hurt me the worst," he continued, "was that I was taught to repress my feelings. Anger. Resentment. Sex. I wasn't supposed to express myself at all. Just be a numb, dumb little fundy. When I got away, I decided to dump it and let everything hang out. I did some things that I thought wouldn't bother me. But I found you can't erase what was branded on your conscience in childhood. Now I'm not sure what I want for myself. I'm bored when I'm good and miserable when I'm bad."

Others in their late teens and early twenties gave similar accounts. Some came only a few times, then vanished in the anonymity of the city. Those who stayed joined the voices asking for new styles of faith and worship within the Elm-LaSalle fellowship.

They couldn't see, for example, why applicants for membership had to sign a pledge to abstain from the five celebrated fundamentalist taboos—movies, card playing, dancing, smoking, and drinking.

"All I suggest is that you be honest," Bill told 16 new candidates for membership. Fourteen noted after the movie clause that they intended to continue seeing selected pictures.

Bill sent the applications to the Moody Church membership committee. The 14 movie dissenters were rejected.

Bill took the applications back to the committee in person:

"As your youth minister, I got to know your young people pretty well. Most of them, and I would guess also many older members of this church, see an occasional movie, despite the pledge they signed. You've rejected these 14 people just because they're honest enough to tell you in advance what they plan to do."

"Well, if Bill will promise to keep an eye on them, I'm for accepting them," one member said. The others grudgingly relented and went along with this condition.

More young adults kept joining Elm-LaSalle, until the balance was tipped against the blue-collar whites. More MBI employees from the neighborhood had moved because of high rents in private housing and high crime around the Cabrini-Green project. Unhappy and uncomfortable with the direction Elm-LaSalle was taking, they found it "inconvenient" to drive back to the old neighborhood for services.

Attendance, however, was actually increasing. The tutoring, changed to Monday night, and after-school activities for neighborhood youth had convinced black parents that a new day had dawned in the little church that had been off-limits to their race for over 80 years. Sunday mornings in 1965 the building was jammed with children. The fellowship hall was a literal Babel as a dozen teachers presided over their flocks around rectangular tables with only screens between them.

In racial makeup the Sunday school and worship service were reversed. The Sunday school was 90 percent black; the worship hour 90 percent white. But while it didn't seem that the ratio in Sunday school was going to change soon, Bill anticipated that black participation in worship would grow.

The civil rights revolution was now in full bloom. American involvement in Vietnam was growing but was yet to divide the country. College campuses were alive with rallies for racial justice. "Going south to help Dr. King" was in. The students attending Elm-LaSalle were eager to help. They dreamed with Martin Luther King of a time when "this nation will rise up and live out the true meaning of its creed: 'We hold these truths to be self-evident, that all men are created equal.' "

The most vociferous one continued to be Gene Brack. He joined the civil rights march from Montgomery to Selma. His friends at Elm-LaSalle saw him a few days later in the television news, his white face bobbing in the front lines near King. Brack returned to Chicago but did not go back to Elm-LaSalle. He took a job as midwestern editor of the show business organ, *Billboard Magazine*.

56

Civil rights was also hot at Garrett-Northwestern when Bill completed his Master's in May, 1965. His thesis was on "The Concept of Assurance of Salvation in the Writings of Paul." In the fall he finally began seminar and class work for his Ph.D.

His professors and fellow students were decrying the failure of institutional churches to face up to racism. They were deriding fundamentalists for inaction. It was time, they said, that Christians lived up to their profession of love.

Bill agreed with his friends in graduate school that fundamentalist congregations were lacking in social conscience and that some were actually racist. But he felt that some of his Methodist friends were derelict in accepting the authority of Scripture and the necessity of a vital personal relationship with God.

"We need both the horizontal and the vertical," he told the new young-adult leadership at Elm-LaSalle.

So they spent hour upon hour in small groups and on church retreats in Wisconsin discussing the question, What should the Church be? In sum, they decided that members should be individually committed to God through the redemptive work of Christ, bound to one another in a caring body of believers, and joined together in a whole-person ministry to people in the community.

This meant getting more deeply involved with the diverse peoples who lived around the church.

Bill, Chuck Hogren, and a few others were already waist-deep in human problems that seemed insolvable. Chuck and his roommate Dave Goodson, for example, had taken Jake, the alcoholic panhandler, into their home for six months with little apparent effect. The families of some of the children being tutored caused even more frustration. The drinking, fighting, and loose sex were appalling to Chuck and Bill who had been raised on white, middle-class morality. Some of the requests for advice were mind-boggling, such as the young girl who asked Bill, "What am I to do when I come home and find my momma making out with a stranger on the living room couch?"

Most of the kids were from two to four years behind their assigned

57

grades in school. It was disappointing to ask a boy what he wanted to be and hear him answer, "A pimp like Harry. That dude travels in style."

The local schools were shocking. Younger kids were beaten up by older ones for the few coins they might have. Teachers presided over the chaos of pupils hurling insults and curses at one another. The odor of marijuana permeated rest rooms and stairwells. Outside, the kids could only play in the streets and garbage-strewn alleys.

The weekday youth program had to be drastically revamped. The Bible club and Vacation Bible School materials prepared for small-town and suburban middle-class white children did not relate. Elm-LaSalle put the emphasis on wholesome recreation and skill-building. Four nights and two afternoons a week the downstairs was jammed with neighborhood kids. Saturdays there were field trips and Sunday afternoons, swimming and basketball at the nearby Lawson YMCA's youth building.

The Sunday afternoon recreation was not greeted with cheers by some of the older members of Elm-LaSalle and the Moody Church board who felt that the first day of the week should not be "profaned." The Sunday prohibitions had bothered Bill when he was directing the summer Moody youth camps. The rules said no swimming, boating, or organized play on Sunday. The kids had to sit around between services in the sweltering heat watching youths from adjoining camps splash and frolic in the cool water. Unable to get the rules changed, Bill had to turn the hoses on them to cool them off.

The Elm-LaSalle board did not want to increase tensions with Moody Church, but they felt the positive outweighed the negative. Sunday was the only day of the week when they could have the "Y" youth building exclusively to themselves; the manager even gave them their own key. And the young adults felt that legalistic rules should bend to the needs of black youth who had little else to do but roam the streets.

The mother church board was also unhappy over evening goings-on in the Elm-LaSalle church building. One passerby reported dancing. What he saw through a window was the silhouette of a black teenager swaying to rock music from a transistor radio held in his hand. As busy and pressured as Bill was, he had to go and explain that to the board.

Bill and the young adults felt it was time to press for independence from Moody Church. Actually, the branch church had been paying its own way since Jim Johnson's time. But an old debt of about $5,000 was still on the books.

Because of the sensitive feelings, Bill suggested that the church seek independence in three successive stages—finances, membership, and finally the purchase of the building.

He challenged Elm-LaSalle attenders to increase their giving to pay off the debt. This wasn't easy. Thirty percent of the student membership turned over every year. And the young doctors were barely paid survival wages by the hospitals that employed them as interns and residents. But in 1966 the debt was erased and the Elm-LaSalle board formally asked the Moody Church board for a separate bank account. This request was granted.

Suddenly a mini-tornado hit on the housing front. The newspapers reported that a Chicago realtor had bought a plot of land behind the church seven blocks long and three blocks wide. An expensive chain motel was to be built on the site between expanding Old Town and the downtown Loop.

Most old housing on the plot was occupied by black families whose incomes were not quite low enough to qualify for residence in Cabrini-Green. Fearing higher rents if they had to move, and desiring to remain in the old neighborhood, they rallied community opposition against the motel. There were reports that the developer was spreading money around. This could not be proven, but a local black politician did tell Bill that he had refused a $10,000 offer to "calm the people down."

While the controversy continued to rage, eviction notices went out and bulldozers cleared the land. In one month Elm-LaSalle lost 26 families. That the city finally vetoed the plans seemed a hollow victory.

It was a difficult time for Bill and Adrienne. Bill's schedule and the long hours of separation were putting strains on their marriage. Because Adrienne seldom was able to come to church, except on Sunday mornings, many did not know she was Bill's wife. One admiring fellow failed to notice her wedding ring and asked for a date. When she replied, ''I'm the pastor's wife,'' he blushed crimson.

Adrienne's interests were mainly in Wheaton. Besides caring for the house and the children, she had begun teaching art classes at the Franklin Elementary School in Wheaton, and two weekly Bible classes met at her home.

One class of neighborhood women met on a weekday. The other class for students, which was taught by a local businessman, met on a week night. Busy in the city, Bill was not aware that the students' class had been moved to another night. One evening when he called home, the businessman, who had arrived early with another friend to go over his outline, answered the phone. Hearing a strange male voice irritated Bill. But when he asked for Adrienne and was told she was soaking in the bathtub, he almost blew his cool. ''What's going on?'' he demanded.

Another strain was their widening disagreement over political issues and social problems in the city. Adrienne was a conservative Republican who fretted with Wheaton neighbors over welfare cheats. Bill, who now saw himself as a political independent, was distressed over the agonies of the poor and dispossessed. He feared that a conservative in the presidency might cut off federally funded programs for urban poor. Adrienne was not so concerned. As the Goldwater-Johnson campaign progressed, the tension between the Leslies heightened. Eventually they declared a truce, but the division in outlook remained.

At least Adrienne was happy in Wheaton with her suburban life. Bill didn't seem to belong anywhere—not with the Protestant liberals who scoffed at the inspiration of the Bible and other cherished doctrines nor with the theological conservatives who appeared to have drawn a curtain of uncaring isolation around themselves. And now it seemed he could not make Adrienne understand the troubles of his soul.

One morning during summer Vacation Bible School, a man burst into a meeting. "Johnny, Harry," he called, "you'd better come home. Your old man has been shot." Bill went to the hospital and found the father paralyzed from the waist down. He had been shot for refusing a $5 loan.

After the man was brought back to his family, Bill was called to the apartment one night. "George tried to kill me, Reverend," the wife moaned. "Can't you pray or do something?" Bill did all that he could do.

A few weeks later Bill was contacted again. The oldest boy in the family and his girl friend had quarreled. Handing her his loaded gun, he dared her to shoot. A friend present said, "If you're going to play like that, I'm going home." She turned and shot the friend.

The tale of horror wasn't done yet.

A married member of the family went out one morning to get milk for his baby and was robbed and killed. A cousin's house burned in February, and Bill found the family living under the open sky in zero weather.

Such suffering and tragedy were almost more than Bill could bear. He walked the streets around the old church questioning the love of a God who would allow such misery. Sometimes he sat in his tiny church office, wondering how long he could keep his sanity.

In his Gethsemane of the mid-60s one of his few diversions was listening to sports contests on the radio. One winter evening he was driving home to Wheaton and caught the closing minutes of a close Ohio State-Michigan basketball game. Being a native of Ohio, Bill was pulling for Ohio State. The lead rocked back and forth to a razor-edge finish, and when Ohio State won, he gave a cheer of victory.

When he got home, Adrienne was already in bed. He switched on the television, only to find a delayed telecast of the game. For a few moments he sat with eyes glued on the screen, his body tensing each time Ohio State lost the lead. Suddenly he leaned back and laughed out loud. "Why am I getting so uptight?" he asked himself. "I already know how it's going to end."

The analogy hit with the next thought. "Why am I so worried about

61

my reputation and the church? God has told me how it's going to end.''

A refreshing peace swept over him.

Crisis of Conscience

5

Crisis of Conscience

JAMES BALDWIN HAD PREDICTED: "When a race riot occurs . . . it will not spread merely to Birmingham . . . [but] to every metropolitan center in the nation which has a significant Negro population."

The first big explosion hit the Watts area of Los Angeles. Thirty-four persons died, hundreds were injured, and whole blocks of businesses were looted and burned. After Watts, other cities went off like a string of giant firecrackers. The disorders were not truly race riots but were each, as the McCone Commission described Watts, "a formless, quite senseless, all but hopeless, violent protest—engaged in by a few, but bringing great distress to all."

While the ghettos of Los Angeles, Newark, Detroit and other cities burned, Chicago remained moderately calm. Some thought the Windy City would stay peaceful. A sizable black middle-class lived on the south side. Blacks played a part in Mayor Daley's machine; indeed, the black vote had provided his winning margin in the last election. And the Chicago police were the toughest in the land. So they said.

But Bill Leslie, Chuck Hogren, and others close to the frustrations in the housing projects and slum tenements knew the fuse was burning in Chicago. Yet they felt there was still time if those who could would help.

Elm-LaSalle was ready to jump into the fray, but lacked financial reserves to fund needed programs. The young adults were eager to devote time and effort, but the money would have to come from outside.

Wes Hartsell, an Evangelical newspaperman, and Cliff Michaelson, a sales manager of a candy company, talked to their home congregation, the South Park Church in suburban Park Ridge. South Park, an independent congregation, became the first church to send regular financial support to Elm-LaSalle.

Dr. Arthur Volle, Bill's former landlord in Wheaton, went through his church's directory and marked the names of persons he thought would be responsive. Letters were sent and some made donations.

Jim Johnson was back from graduate studies at Michigan State and serving as director of the Wheaton-based Evangelical Literature Overseas. Prospecting at a large suburban Bible church, one of the largest givers to foreign missions in fundamentalism, Johnson suggested that the least suburban Christians could do was help a church on the front line of ministry in the turbulent inner city.

The attitude toward the city and social problems at many churches in Wheaton was so negative that some students from the college stopped attending. One group gathered on Sunday morning in a local restaurant for discussions about what might be done to effect change. A number of students at the Evangelical Free Church's Trinity College and Divinity School in north suburban Bannockburn also chafed for action. Even at the more placid Moody Bible Institute there was frustration.

Campus radicalism spread from California across the country, challenging establishment values. The dropout hippie movement was in full bloom. Drug use was rising. Traveling blue-jeaned and sandaled flower children discovered Old Town. College and high school students in the Chicago area came down on weekends to fraternize with the visitors. The aura of the hippie culture enveloped the near north side.

An old vacant brick mansion that had survived the great Chicago fire of 1871 stood kitty-corner across the street from the church. The wealthy owners offered it rent free to Elm-LaSalle; "on condition that you take care of it," they said. The young adults immediately began planning sing-a-longs and other musical entertainment on Saturday nights for counter-culture youth. Bill cautioned that they go easy on the message. "Hold your testimonies to a minute or two between the songs. Let's use what we say to interest people in going on retreats where we can have more time with them."

They invited a variety of both sacred and secular performers. Suzanne Johnson, the current Miss Illinois, gave a concert. Win Stracke brought students from his Old Town School of Folk Music to sing his ballad about the local 42nd ward. The song had lines about the police, the merchants, the hippies, Cabrini-Green, and even Moody Church. It said, "Moody Church may be full on Sunday but doesn't care what happens at Wells and North on Saturday." Bill felt the judgment was too severe and wished the words had not been sung. But it was too late and only served to widen the gap between Elm-LaSalle and Moody Church.

One evening a Christian rock group called the Crimson Bridge performed. About 20 Puerto Rican youths from the Young Lords gang were in the audience. The plan of the musicians was to present secular songs that raised questions about the meaning of life, then give the Christian answer. The Young Lords soon walked out. When Bill asked them later, "Why did you leave?" one replied, "Man, we got tired of waiting for those phony cats to come out of their bags."

Bill heard that a young Englishman with experience in starting coffeehouses in Britain was at Wheaton College. He invited Ian Kerr to look the neighborhood over.

"Do you think a coffeehouse would go here?" Bill asked him.

"I don't see why not," Kerr replied.

"Then would you like to handle it?"

Kerr grinned his assent.

He went back to Wheaton and recruited 32 students to work with him. On opening night in the fall of '65 "The Extension" was ready. The long Sunday school class tables had been stacked in the room in back of the all-purpose fellowship hall. Borrowed card tables ringed the raised center stage from which musical performances and poetry readings would be given. The tables were papered for creative doodling under the light of candles flickering in colored jars. Guests sat on padded barrels beneath blown-up photographs of contemporary youth celebrities which swayed from the ceiling.

Early in the evening the student staffers strolled through Old Town, passing out invitations. "Guests" followed them down Wells Street and through a dark alley to a black-lighted sign that announced the back-door entrance to The Extension. Each guest paid a fifty-cent cover charge to pay for refreshments and to insure he would stay.

The menu presented the purpose of the coffeehouse: to provide "opportunity for extension of ourselves to one another and to Jesus Christ."

Every hour, cards were circulated with questions, such as "What would it take for you to be happy?" This was to provoke dialogue for the next 20 minutes, after which came a half-hour's entertainment. Bill once more advised the Christian students to go easy and work up to direct witnessing. The students disagreed, saying, "These people don't want to play word games. They want to know right off what we think about life."

Then Bill remembered what the Young Lord gang members had told him about the rock concert. "Go ahead," he said. "You understand the youth culture better than I do."

Through the fall, winter, and spring hundreds of youths received free modern-language New Testaments and heard testimonies from their peers. Many of the newly converted traveled on to give their witness in other cities. One Elm-LaSalle member who moved to California wrote back that she had run into three people who said they had been introduced to Christ at The Extension.

Graduate school and the stepped-up program at Elm-LaSalle continued to keep Bill busy. He seldom attended the board meetings at Moody Church anymore. His attitude reflected the majority feeling of Elm-LaSalle toward the mother church: "Let them go their way and we'll go ours."

Meanwhile, Moody Church faced their own problems. For four

years after Redpath left, they lacked pastoral leadership. They had interim pastors, but only part time. A steady parade of prominent guest speakers hadn't checked the declining attendance. Finally, in 1966, they installed a new pastor. But the exodus to the suburbs, which had begun even before Redpath left, now continued in force. The resulting drain in finances put extreme pressures on the church.

Impeccably groomed, with distinguished-looking silver hair, Dr. George Sweeting had once studied at the Art Institute of Chicago. He was a fundamentalist in doctrine but no ultra-separatist—a good friend of Billy Graham and other "New Evangelicals."

Sweeting believed it was high time that Biblical conservatives came out of the woodwork. In a sermon titled "The City: A Matter of Conscience," he charged that Evangelicals had been withdrawing from cities "for many years." This, he said, was "part of a general retreat from the world," explaining,

> Evangelical Christians often equate their faith with nice people, blue skies, smiles, and upper-class goals. In rural America the . . . conservative Protestant is dominant. His attitudes and style of life set the tone for the whole society—the respectable standard—the American way. But in the city the Protestant is a distinct minority . . . [and his] life-style is not dominant. . . .

> The majority of Evangelicals have long held an anti-city attitude, associating the city with Sodom and Gomorrah, scarlet women, crime, and filth. This anti-urban bias . . . is suicidal to the church of Jesus Christ.

> This is in no way an endorsement of the "social gospel." Rather I am pleading for a Christian awareness of practical day-to-day needs of people, as we share with them what Christ can do. Although we do this on the mission field, we often neglect the neighbors almost at our back door.

What specifically did Sweeting think could be done?

> We can experiment. We can try direct mail to individuals who live

> in the high-rise apartments. We can begin young adult clubs, home
> Bible study classes, Bible education programs. A family or indi-
> vidual can move into an apartment building and be a "light" shining
> in darkness, or "salt" flavoring its environment.

Sweeting soon became aware of the strained relation with the little branch congregation down the street. Someone presented him with a beer can that had been found on the piano in the fellowship hall. At the complainer's insistence, he called Bill Leslie. Bill explained that they tried to police the young people attending the various functions, but with so many coming and going it was impossible to guard each at every moment. Sweeting smiled and said he understood.

Sweeting put Moody Church back on the upswing. Then he turned his attention to Elm-LaSalle, which wanted to buy its building and become independent. He talked with some board members, then called Bill to his office and suggested that $15,000 would be sufficient, although the building was worth at least $90,000. Bill remembered he had earlier told the Moody Church board that it was customary for a branch church to buy its building for a token $1. But he didn't argue. "I'll recommend the $15,000 figure to our board," he promised Sweeting. "But I can't guarantee anything."

The Elm-LaSalle board turned down the offer. "Fifteen thousand will put us out of business," Chairman Roy Mitchell declared. "Moody Church should give us the building. Their budget for a week is more than we pay you in a year, Bill."

Then they voted, over Bill's counsel, to offer a token one dollar for the building. The Moody Church board wasted no time in saying no.

The impasse with Moody Church and the isolation of Elm-LaSalle from other Evangelicals bothered Bill. Deep down he began worrying that the church might have gone off balance in social programs.

During this time of soul-searching, Evangelical missionary leaders were holding a congress on missions at Wheaton College. After reaffirming belief in fundamental Biblical doctrines, they urged "all Evangelicals to stand openly and firmly for racial equality, human freedom, and all forms of social justice throughout the world." They did not, however, spell out specific ways in which Evangelicals should become socially involved.

Near the end of the congress, several key participants took part in a panel discussion over WBBM, the 50,000-watt CBS radio outlet in Chicago. Bill happened to hear the program as he was driving home to Wheaton.

Moderator Jerry Williams began by asking why the panel members didn't cooperate with the World Council of Churches.

"Oh, the World Council is concerned with social work, and we are interested in the spiritual," one replied.

"Don't you care about poverty, hunger, and racial discrimination?"

The panel unanimously insisted that they did care, but as one put it, "Our main job is to help people find a personal relationship with God."

The discussion shifted to foreign missions. "What are you doing abroad?" Williams asked.

Clyde Taylor, General Director of the National Association of Evangelicals, launched into a glowing description of medical and educational ministries. When he finished, the moderator commented astutely, "Apparently you are practicing overseas what you are leaving for others to do here."

"We're on the right path after all," Bill practically shouted as he drove along.

But to still lingering doubts he made a fresh study of the Bible and modern church history on social justice and ministry.

He saw how God had instructed Israel to care for "strangers" and to leave grain in the fields for gleaners. He noted that every 50th year in Israel was a Year of Jubilee. Debts were canceled, ancestral lands restored to their families, and slaves freed. He read the scalding remarks of the Old Testament prophets against establishment injustice—Isaiah 1:23, for example: "Your princes are rebels and companions of thieves. Every one loves a bribe and runs after gifts. They do not defend the fatherless, and the widow's cause does not come to them" (RSV). He perused the philosophic writings and was amazed at the numerous references to social righteousness, such as Proverbs 16:8, 11: "Better is a little with righteousness than great revenues with injustice. . . . A just balance and scales are the Lord's."

He read through the Gospels, marveling at Jesus' identification with the poor and oppressed. The Messiah's charter of ministry in Luke 4: 18, 19 intrigued him: "The Spirit of the Lord is upon me, because he has anointed me to preach good news to the poor. He has sent me to proclaim release to the captives and recovering of sight to the blind, to set at liberty those who are oppressed . . . ." And Matthew 25 reminded him that disciples actually ministered to Jesus by feeding the hungry, giving drink to the thirsty, welcoming the homeless, clothing the naked, helping the sick, and visiting the prisoners.

Likewise the Epistles. Paul had received an offering from the Macedonian believers for the poor saints in Jerusalem. He had instructed the young minister Timothy to "charge them [the rich] not to be haughty, nor to set their hopes on uncertain riches but on God who richly furnishes us with everything to enjoy. They are to do good, to be rich in good deeds, liberal and generous, thus laying up for themselves a good foundation for the future . . . ." James had asked, "What does it profit, my brethren, if a man says he has faith but has not works? Can his faith save him? If a brother or sister is ill-clad and in lack of daily food, and one of you says to them, 'Go in peace, be warmed and filled,' without giving them the things needed for the body, what does it profit? So faith by itself, if it has no works, is dead." And John had warned, "But if any one has the world's goods and sees his brother in need, yet closes his heart against him, how does God's love abide in him? Little children, let us not love in word or speech but in deed and in truth."

Skipping across the centuries to modern times, Bill noted that English and American Evangelicals in the 17th, 18th, and 19th centuries had been in the forefront of crusades for such social reforms as the humane treatment of prisoners and the abolition of slavery. The great names whom fundamentalists loved to quote had been intimately involved with helping poor people. George Muller had fed thousands of orphans. Pulpiteers Charles H. Spurgeon and T. DeWitt Talmadge had helped establish employment bureaus, feeding centers, and other agencies to help the poor. Charles G. Finney's revivals had provided the atmosphere for the growth of numerous benevolent societies. The conclusion was obvious: before the 20th century, social welfare and evangelism had not been separated. The turning point had come with the fundamentalist-modernist controversy over theology and the Social Gospel.

Bill's call for the recovery of a "balanced Gospel" was well received by the young congregation. His preaching, along with the freedom of inquiry and sharing, made Elm-LaSalle the "in" church for students and recent Christian college graduates who felt restricted in fundamentalist churches.

Bill presented new members to the church with glowing introductions. For instance, he presented Nancy Board as "secretary to the dean of the University of Chicago Law School." Actually, she was secretary to only *a* dean of students there. Moving on to the next person, he said, "We're proud to have Cameron Webb, head of the credit department at Harris Bank." The embarrassed Webb was only a credit investigator.

"Employed" members were a minority in contrast to the students who were subsisting on fellowship grants, intern salaries, and part-time jobs. Most of the financial supporters of the early '60s had moved away. Only six remained from those welcoming Bill in 1961.

Still, with gifts from South Park Church and a few individual outside supporters, finances were slowly increasing. Stable, professional leadership was more critically needed. Bill finally decided to approach some talented Evangelicals who were living in the city.

Omer Reese had sung in the Elm-LaSalle choir while a student at MBI in the '50s. Afterward, he had earned a degree from the American Conservatory of Music and had been a paid soloist in two large Chicago churches. He now taught music at a high school and was a section leader in the Chicago Chorus. His wife, Beverly, a graduate of Bob Jones, was a teacher in inner-city schools.

Omer was indifferent to Bill's plea "to come and help us build a music program."

"I'm afraid your kind of music wouldn't be our bag," Omer said frankly. "The little choruses, the same old 19th-century hymns, the Sunday night bit where you're supposed to make everyone feel like singing. I've had it with that circuit."

"So have I," Bill said. "That's why I called you."

"No, it wouldn't work."

"Well, will you at least think and pray about it?" Bill persisted.

The Reeses did—and a few weeks later came to help.

Omer felt as Bill did that the traditional Evangelical service was doing little to help people worship. The minister in his prayer, Scripture reading, and sermon did most of the talking to God while the people sat mute. The hymns were addressed more to the people (testimonials, calls to serve, proclamation of doctrine, and so on) than to God. And much of the music accompaniment followed frontier camp-meeting patterns of harmony and rhythm.

Slowly, experimentally, but determinedly, Bill and Omer began shaping the service to facilitate meeting with God, individually and corporately.

Other, more obvious changes were made in the order of activities. The Wednesday evening prayer meeting was dropped in favor of home groups. Sunday school was moved back to 9:00 a.m. on Sunday morning, with worship following at 10:00, and a Fellowship Hour at 11:00. The traditional Sunday evening evangelistic service gave way to a more formal vespers.

The nine o'clock Sunday school proved impractical. It was hard to get neighborhood children out of bed after they had stayed up to watch the 4:00 a.m. movie. They had to be fed breakfast at the church. And for young parents with preschool children, three hours was too long a time. The Leslies left home at 7:30 and did not return until 2:30.

They changed the schedule again, putting Sunday school and worship simultaneously at ten. School-age children joined their parents for worship preliminaries, then moved downstairs for their classes. The adult education sessions were shifted to Sunday evening and called "forums." The college-level forums centered on a seminar-type topical study and vespers were dropped.

Marjorie Branch, the black woman who with her brother had integrated Moody Church, was invited to become Elm-LaSalle's Director of Christian Education. Branch was then heading up a federally financed program in school-community relations in the Chicago school system. She accepted on the condition that the $25 a week allotted to the part-time position be used to hire older neighborhood youth to help in church recreation programs. "It isn't much, but it will be something," she said. "Kids in this neighborhood don't have the opportunities for baby-sitting and other jobs which middle-class youth do."

Marj Branch noted that Elm-LaSalle was involved with three types of youth. The white hippies came to the coffeehouse on weekends. Lower-middle-class kids, mostly black, came to Sunday school. Youths from the more distant Cabrini-Green Housing Project participated in the weekday recreation and skill-building programs. The latter were mostly from fatherless, black, welfare families.

She opposed the busing of black children in from Cabrini-Green for Sunday school. "That will just further fragment their families," she said. "Besides, this isn't their turf and there might be trouble. Blacks living in private housing consider Cabrini-Green blacks 'field niggers.' "

The bulldozers continued to rumble throughout the neighborhood. More giant high rises had sprung up to the east and north of the church. The Carl Sandburg development, just three blocks to the northeast, covered four blocks and housed 7,000 people. But few neighborhood families could afford to live in Sandburg Village or one of the other new high rises.

Land was now being cleared under the name of urban renewal. The idea was that the city would take title to the land and build new, durable housing for local residents. But in other areas of Chicago, urban renewal had meant people removal with only the well-to-do able to pay the rents.

Rumors abounded that developers with good political connections were cleaning up on the near-north side. There was deep community resentment over what was happening. The realtors, investment bank ers, and their political cronies seemed to get richer. The affluent could enjoy cool lake breezes and the convenience of living near the downtown Loop, while low-income people who had grown up in the area had to find housing in decaying neighborhoods further out or an apartment in crime-infested Cabrini-Green.

Neighborhood feelings also ran strong against Moody Bible Institute. The Institute had cleared old housing from two blocks, forcing the residents to look elsewhere, and had turned the property into parking lots and student tennis courts. Local people felt the property could have been developed better for low-income housing. They did not understand that Moody, with a growing enrollment, needed the facilities to stay in the city.

Neighbors were further upset over MBI'S refusal to allow their children to use the school's gym. When MBI claimed insurance problems, someone pointed out that children of faculty members and employees were using the gym. Whether true or not, blacks charged that the real reason was racism.

While tensions kept building in the neighborhood, one of Bill Leslie's closest minister friends was seeking a new niche of service in the city. As befitted custom, David Mains, whom Bill had recommended as youth minister at Moody Church, had resigned upon the arrival of a new head pastor. Mains had been frustrated to the point of having tension headaches on Saturday afternoon in anticipation of the Sunday services. "There were occasions in the repetitious absurdity of services," Mains later wrote in his book *Full Circle*, "when I wanted to stand up and scream at the top of my lungs just to have broken the futility of it all."

For the young ex-YFC evangelist the last months of 1966 were a time of agonizing reappraisal. Bill Leslie had been responsible for bringing him into city work, and it was to Bill that he went for brotherly support. But Bill could only pray with him and say that he understood his travail of soul.

As David talked with Bill and other friends and read every book he could find on church renewal, the idea gradually came that he and his wife Karen should start a new church in the city instead of accepting one of the suburban pastorates he had been offered. They would begin in an area like Elm-LaSalle where the generations, races, and social classes daily crossed paths. By the end of 1966, the Mains had found 50 friends who shared their vision. They focused on the near-west side, about four miles from Elm-LaSalle, and by a miracle of sorts obtained permission to meet free in a large auditorium owned by Local 705 of the Teamsters Union.

Their first service was scheduled for the first Sunday in February, 1967. On Thursday and Friday the city was paralyzed with 36 inches of snow. Nevertheless, 28 people braved the climax of the "storm of the century" to launch the new Circle Church.

David and Karen Mains, like Bill and Adrienne Leslie, were children of the fundamentalist faithful. David's parents were pillars in the Wheaton Evangelical Free Church. Karen's father was head of the music department at Moody Bible Institute and her mother was a well-known Christian poet. It was disconcerting to fundamentalist elders that some of their best and brightest young people were flocking to Elm-LaSalle and Circle churches. But in Bill Leslie and David Mains the students found leaders who were open to change and speaking prophetically to the tumultuous times in which they lived.

They would need such leaders during the troubled days that were soon to come.

The Threat

6

The Threat

ELM-LASALLE was spared the worst of the long hot summer of '67. Over 100 were killed, 200 injured, and $100 million in property damage incurred in 41 major riots across the country. But not in Chicago. Mayor Daley's lakeside metropolis remained relatively quiet, although there was no relaxation of tensions. No one was yet willing to predict that Chicago would be spared the fire and the fury.

Elm-LaSalle was located right in the middle of potential conflict, with blacks behind the church and whites in front. Sundays, the church was integrated, but the rest of the week it generally was not. No signs said one race should keep out on certain nights. It was simply that the church had the coffeehouse for college students on Friday and Saturday, and most collegians were white. Other nights were for elementary and high school students, and they were mostly black.

A residual of the old guard that didn't approve of the social programs still remained. But their patience was running short.

The ornate pool table was the last straw.

It was purchased at a bargain price of $200 from a Methodist layman in suburban Oak Park who had been giving money to the youth programs. They put the old antique, refinished with coats of varnish until it shone, in the little room behind the fellowship hall. The neighborhood kids loved it.

But the conservatives saw it as a symbol of all they had opposed in the years past. The leader, a long-time member of the Elm-LaSalle board, handed Bill an ultimatum: "Either that thing goes or we go."

Bill felt that the man's strong feelings stemmed partly from recent tragedies his family had experienced. He was sick of being buffeted by change, and now the one secure institution in his life, his church, had, in his thinking, turned away from the old paths.

Still Bill could not give in to the view of the group that had once been a majority. "No, I can't tell the kids we're taking it out just because some of our members don't like it. They wouldn't understand. And I don't believe it would be right."

"Very well," the protester replied. "We'll be leaving."

It was another hard blow. The former board member, his wife, and their friends had been faithful workers and financial supporters. Even with their help Elm-LaSalle had just been scraping by. Bill's $100 weekly salary had often been late. He had only a partial scholarship to help pay his graduate school tuition. Only Adrienne's teaching salary, loans from a bank, and insurance policies kept the family afloat.

But there was no time to worry about finances. Every minute of Bill's time seemed to be taken.

For one thing, he or Chuck had to be at the church almost every night to keep order. "Never threaten them," Marj Branch had advised. "Just tell them what you expect, and if they don't measure up, then take action."

A loser at pool was expected to sit down and give someone else a chance to play. On this particular night Chuck was meeting with the church education committee when he heard a commotion in the billiard room.

He rushed into the room, asking, "What's the difficulty?"

"Harold Brown won't give up his cue stick," a skinny boy complained.

Chuck knew Harold well. He lived immediately behind the church and seemed to always be in trouble with the police. Once Chuck had been driving the boys to a picnic and noticed a police car following. They were just keeping a suspicious eye on Harold. Another time police had picked Harold up for cashing a stolen check. Harold claimed he was just doing a friend a favor. Chuck had gone to bat for him at the police station.

"You know the rules, Harold," Chuck said.

"Yeah, but I won. This cat's tryin' to say I lost."

"OK, let me decide. One at a time, each of you tell me your side of the argument."

When they finished, Chuck decreed that Harold had lost and should sit down. But instead of accepting this decision, the 14-year-old bull of a boy slammed Chuck to the floor. At that moment a huge black teacher ran into the room. The teacher, Columbus Salley, had also been meeting with the education committee.

"Get off Chuck!" he demanded.

"No!" Harold shouted back. "He said I lost and I didn't!"

Salley reached down with a brawny arm, picked up the boy, and pushed him against the wall. "Are you going to stop?"

"No!" Harold screamed.

Salley threw him against the wall again and again and again until the overgrown boy cried, "OK, OK, I've had enough. I'm sorry I jumped on Chuck."

Chuck extended his hand. "Forget it. We're friends."

A much more serious incident took place in the coffeehouse a few weeks later. Tom Skinner, the young, black evangelist who had led a gang in Harlem before his conversion, was to speak that Friday evening at Moody Church. Bill had invited several black high school students to meet early at Elm-LaSalle and go together in a van to hear Skinner. They arrived ahead of Bill, while the Wheaton students were still decorating the fellowship hall.

One of the blacks stepped inside to see what was happening. "Hey, guys," he called back to his friends. "Come see what these dudes are doin'."

The blacks poured in. It was the first time they had seen the fellowship hall fixed up for the college crowd.

The Wheaton students entered into friendly banter with them and all went well until a white girl addressed a black as "nigger." She said it in innocence. The blacks had been using the term freely. But coming from a white it was an insult.

The offended black threw a punch at a white youth. The white raised an arm to defend himself. Another black jumped a barrel chair to enter the fray. Within seconds a full-scale melee was on. Tables were turned over, and napkins and table decorations went flying. Bill ran in and began pulling blacks off surprised Wheaton students, trying to calm things down. Finally he got the blacks out and into the van. He took them on to Moody Church, but none seemed to show any interest in what Tom Skinner was saying.

Now that the blacks had discovered The Extension they began coming regularly. The local blacks were for the most part respectful of Bill and Chuck. It was strange blacks from the west and south sides that wouldn't listen to a reminder that only those who behaved were welcome. They came in high on drugs or wine and had to be told to leave. Any who balked were taken by the arm and hustled out the door, usually by Bill because he had the strongest grip. It was a standing joke that if Bill quit preaching he could work as a bouncer in a night club.

By the fall of 1967 the extent of the racial crisis was beginning to dawn on white Americans. But most Evangelicals continued to be defensive and reactionary. Many blamed the racial strife on "communist revolutionaries," incited by such firebrands as Stokely Carmichael and Rap Brown. Even Martin Luther King, the hero of civil rights, was categorized as a communist or a Red sympathizer. Some blatantly declared that churches such as Elm-LaSalle were paying too much attention to the inner-city poor and racial minorities. As one prominent Evangelical put it in a major address in September, 1967, "With all the clamor about the poor and minorities in our society, it's time someone speaks up in defense of white Anglo-Saxon Protestant Puritans. I'm for the upper dog."

On February 29, 1968, the National Advisory Commission on Civil Disorders, appointed by President Lyndon Johnson, issued its findings to the nation. The Commission's conclusion: "Our nation is moving toward two societies, one black, one white—separate and unequal." It further declared:

Segregation and poverty have created in the racial ghetto a destructive environment totally unknown to most white Americans.

What white Americans have never fully understood—but what the Negro can never forget—is that white society is deeply implicated in the ghetto. White institutions created it, white institutions maintain it, and white society condones it.

The Commission, composed of nationally respected black and white leaders, called for "strategies for action" that would eliminate minority barriers to jobs, education, and housing; create new jobs to ease the economic conditions of the hard-core unemployed; provide tax incentives to investment in poverty areas; and expand and reorient the urban renewal program to make available six million units of decent housing for the poor.

Bill felt that the Elm-LaSalle neighborhood was a microcosm of all the problems ailing urban America. If something could be done here, there was hope for the cities. If not, then the future looked bleak indeed. Surely the Gospel had something to say to the racial crisis.

Elm-LaSalle had not been alone in attempting to provide solutions for neighborhood problems. Several other churches in the vicinity—notably Catholic, Methodist, Presbyterian, and Lutheran—had launched individual and cooperative efforts in health care, education, housing, food and clothing distribution, and employment. Additionally, about a dozen secular agencies, some receiving government funding, were active.

With so many hands trying to help, an umbrella coordinating organization was needed. This was the Near North Area Council (NNAC). Bill played a major role in keeping its various factions working together, constantly pointing out the need to speak with a unified voice.

The building of Montgomery Ward's $68 million national headquarters at Larrabee Street and Chicago Avenue was a prime example. Bill accompanied a committee of representatives from the various organizations to see Ward's contractor. They requested that he hire one-third of his construction force from the community.

85

"Who do you represent?" he demanded. A committee member handed over a list of member organizations, and the negotiations resulted in scores of jobs for neighborhood unemployed.

The NNAC wanted to elect Bill its president. He declined, feeling the leader should be a black. He did accept the position of vice-president, however.

Such participation did not enhance Bill's reputation with Evangelical conservatives who disapproved of alliances with "unbelievers" and "religious liberals." Bill understood the position of the separatists. He had once felt himself that passages such as II Corinthians 6: 14-17 ("Be ye not unequally yoked together with unbelievers . . .") forbade organizational ties with groups not of Evangelical persuasion. But while at Pekin in 1956 he had decided that fundamentalists had "gone to seed" on separation. He had been repelled by harangues against Billy Graham within his own Conservative Baptist Pastors Fellowship and would come home with splitting headaches, vowing to Adrienne, "I'm never going back."

He was only the second pastor of the Pekin church to join the local ministerial alliance, which, ironically, elected him chairman of the social action committee the first day he attended. Then upon giving him the job, they announced that at the previous meeting they had assigned two important tasks to the committee: (1) find homes for Hungarian refugees, and (2) investigate gambling in the county.

The pastors knew from counseling upset wives that gambling was going on. Bill asked the sheriff, chief of police, and chairman of the county board of supervisors to appear before the ministerial council and answer questions. All denied accepting payoffs. But the investigation made Bill something of a public figure in the press, which came from as far away as Chicago to cover the confrontation.

Bill now felt more strongly than ever that Evangelicals needed to change their thinking on separation. Surely individual Christians could cooperate with anyone in matters of community concern. On the corporate level, he saw no reason why Elm-LaSalle could not work with other churches, even Catholic, on nontheological issues. And in the theological area, he felt that acceptance of the inspiration and authority of Scripture and the divinity of Christ was sufficient as a guide to fellowship. The drawing of boundaries on disputed questions such as whether the Great Tribulation would occur before or after the return of Christ seemed ridiculous. He had no time, however, to argue over such matters. He could only say, "This is how I feel," and go on.

The issues at Pekin seemed so simple compared with the pain and frustrations which enveloped Elm-LaSalle. Pekin had also been easier because there he and Adrienne had worked so closely together. She had for all practical purposes been his associate pastor. Now she was confined to Wheaton, except on Sundays and special days. His time was largely spent on the church and the graduate work which continued to drag on. He had completed his class and seminar work for the Ph.D. and was now working on required languages: German, French, Hebrew, and Greek. After that would come five days of written exams, then the dissertation.

Their concerns kept moving apart. They had so little time together. What kept the marriage intact was a strong commitment of love and a certainty that God had brought them together.

Adrienne Andrew had been raised by fundamentalist parents in the Bible Presbyterian Church in St. Louis, where her father was an elder. She was nurtured under the pastorate of Francis Schaeffer, but it was her pastor's wife who had the greatest influence on her life.

Edith Schaeffer made Christian education fun. She would paint beautiful, intriguing picture cards for Vacation Bible School and hold them up for her enraptured students to see as she led them in singing a chorus of "Be careful, little eyes, what you see." She would hold up a giant eye, then ears, hands, and feet for the different verses.

She had created a delightful comic character named Little Addie that fascinated Adrienne. Watching Edith Schaeffer make scenes for the adventures of Little Addie reinforced Adrienne's desire to study art.

She was pursuing this interest at Wheaton College when her mother phoned, requesting her to return home to help entertain a Gospel team that was coming for a weekend. "Your father's going to be gone on a trip, and it's semester break anyway. I really need your help."

Adrienne would have preferred remaining on campus, but she dutifully returned home.

When the boys arrived that Friday evening, Bill Leslie, the preacher for the team, took one look at Adrienne and assured himself, ''This is the girl God wants me to marry. How have I missed her at Wheaton?'' He had never seen anyone so lovely and so lively. He liked her sense of humor and her vivaciousness. When he was alone in his room later, he asked for divine permission to pursue her.

This was quite a change for Bill, now 22, who had had no special romantic interests until this time. Friends had often warned him that his expectations were too high and that he should lower his sights. His stock reply was always, ''God has someone very special for me and I'm going to wait for her.'' Now he was certain he had found the one. They were engaged by Thanksgiving and were married by Wheaton College President V. Raymond Edman in St. Louis in July of the following year.

Adrienne loved being the pastor's wife at Pekin. The Leslies lived in a comfortable frame home near the church and only three blocks from the business district. Because Pekin was a three-shift town, people stopped by the parsonage from early morning to sometimes past midnight. But Adrienne thrived on the entertaining, counseling, teaching, decorating, and other opportunities of service.

Every time they left town for privacy Bill warned her to slow down. She didn't, and had to be hospitalized for exhaustion three times their third year.

The third time she had two convulsions. Their doctor decided she had a brain tumor and sent her to St. Louis for surgery. She and Bill arrived at her parents' home that evening and after retiring to their room had a long, serious talk. The doctor had said if she survived the operation she might lose her sight or hearing or both. They talked about how God had brought them together and their place in His service. Then Bill knelt by the bed and laid hands on her head after the Biblical custom. Quietly he asked God to heal her.

The next morning she entered the hospital. The encephalogram showed no evidence of a tumor. After keeping her a couple of days, the brain specialist said, "Go home. There's nothing wrong with you that a good rest won't cure." Both Bill and Adrienne felt God had performed a miracle.

When they decided that Bill should resume his graduate study, Adrienne's father advised that they build a large house and rent out rooms to Wheaton students. He offered to lend them the money for the down payment.

Decorating and fixing up her first house and tending to daughters Laurel and Lisa, born only two years apart, and baby Andy kept Adrienne busy. The six male college boarders that slept in the back bedrooms were no bother. Adrienne was "happy as a lark." She loved to look through the solid glass wall at her flowers in front and feel the warmth of the southern sun. The view reminded her of her parents' backyard in St. Louis. She enjoyed the patio which adjoined their bedroom and in which a flowering crab was growing through open beams. She felt it could hardly have been designed better.

She also loved her new friends in the neighborhood—young wives with children and house interests like her own—and teaching art to lively, creative suburban children. Everything about her life was enjoyable and beautiful, except for Bill's being gone so much and his growing preoccupation with problems of the city.

Astonishingly, both reached the same conclusion at the same time. If Bill was to continue at Elm-LaSalle, they should move into the city. Adrienne had heard about the terrible schools, the high crime, the congestion. It would be a hard adjustment, but if that was what God and Bill wanted, then that was what she wanted. At least they would try it for a year.

Having made the decision, they told the children they would rent the house in Wheaton and look for a place near the church. Unable to afford an apartment in one of the luxury high rises, and with older private housing continuing to fall to the bulldozers, they couldn't imagine where.

Shortly after New Year's, 1968, they were invited to a dinner party at a home on the north side in honor of Alan Redpath. Their old friend had suffered a partial stroke and been advised by his doctor to resign his pastorate in Scotland. He was now engaged in a less taxing "deeper life" ministry in churches and Bible conferences.

Bob and Mary Louise Niemeyer, the host and hostess, lived on Crilly Court, a quiet, quaint private little street just a block from Lincoln Park and near the lake. They were hardly inside the tastefully decorated, narrow, three-level town house when Adrienne remarked to Bill, "I would love a place like this."

The Niemeyers invited them back for another dinner party the following month. Adrienne was sitting beside the host when he whispered, "I haven't told anyone yet, but I've found out I'm being transferred."

On the way home, Adrienne mentioned this to Bill and asked, "Do you think we could afford it?"

Bill called the next day and found that the rent was extremely reasonable for the area. They could take over the Niemeyers' lease and move in after school was out in late May. But before signing, Adrienne felt they should check with the public school Laurel and Lisa would be entering in the fall. Adrienne called the principal's office and was told to bring the girls' report cards and come in for an interview.

When the procedure was finished, the principal told the parents, "I'd love to have your daughters, but in all fairness I would recommend a private school. I know you'll want them to go on to high school and college. Only a few of our children ever reach high school, and I have to give them private tutoring in math and science."

They investigated private schools in the area and found that all were full for the coming fall term. The principal at the Harris School was kind enough to test them, even though the school's regular evaluator was out. "It would be a shame to send them to public school," he lamented. "They show such great promise. But we simply have no room."

Nevertheless, despite this depressing news, the Leslies signed the lease. "Surely something will turn up," Adrienne said hopefully.

A cold February passed and a windy March blew into a warm April. The first Thursday evening of the month it was raining in Chicago when a news flash shocked the country. Martin Luther King had been assassinated in Memphis.

The bitterness that swept the black ghettos of the big cities soon exploded into mindless violence. This time Chicago was one of the worst hit with 11 dead, 911 injured, 3,965 arrested, and $11 million in damage done mostly on the west side. While the rioting raged, Rumor Central handled 40,000 telephone calls, squelching scare stories, among them reports that two nuns had been lynched by blacks and that Stokely Carmichael had come ashore from a submarine in Lake Michigan.

Elm-LaSalle had scheduled their catered spring banquet at the church for Saturday night, and people kept calling the Leslies asking if it was still on. It was. Bill felt this was not the time to run.

Friday was a terrible day in Chicago. White students were assaulted in high schools. School buses were pelted with rocks and bottles. Driving home Friday evening, Bill could see flames leaping above the tops of buildings on the west side.

Nearer the church, snipers were firing on street traffic from the upper stories of Cabrini-Green. On streets surrounding the housing project, looters were breaking shop windows and emptying shelves. Hearing radio reports, Adrienne became worried about the Niemeyers and called their house. "We can see the light of fires from our back porch," Mary Louise reported. "But we're all right, thank God."

Saturday afternoon the warfare intensified along LaSalle Street. Chuck Hogren and Dave Strong were in the church office phoning to find out who needed transportation to the banquet. Suddenly they heard shooting outside. Chuck ran to the front door, cracked it just enough to glance outside, then hurried back to report, "There must be a hundred National Guardsmen out there. They have the street blocked off and are firing at snipers on the roof of the A & P across the street."

They could hear bullets from the snipers zinging outside the church. Chuck whispered in an understatement typical of his mild manner, "Maybe we'd better call off the banquet. I'll check with the Leslies about switching it to their house."

The Leslies concurred. Adrienne began rearranging furniture and Bill left to pick up the food from the caterer. By borrowing tables and

91

chairs from a nearby funeral home, they managed to accommodate about 75 people, about half the number who had intended coming to the church.

The speaker was former All-American Bob Davenport, known for leading suburban youth on bike marathons called "Wandering Wheels." The trips had proved highly successful in assisting Christian growth. He challenged Elm-LaSalle to develop a Wandering Wheels program for inner-city black youth.

Davenport stayed overnight with the Leslies; then early Sunday morning he and Bill went down in his car to check on the riot damage. They found houses and stores still smoldering behind the church and the windows of other stores smashed, with the shelves stripped bare of goods. The church had not been harmed. Chuck Hogren, Dave Goodson, and Ron Cook (a new assistant pastor) had slept there the night before with buckets of water and fire extinguishers at every window just in case.

In the 10:00 a.m. worship hour Bill preached to a small band of the faithful from Amos 5:24: "Let justice roll down like waters, and righteousness like an everflowing stream." Then Davenport spoke in Fellowship Hour about Wandering Wheels. "Think what it would mean to inner-city kids to go on such an adventure," he said. "Fresh air, comradeship, and the thrill of reaching a goal. All you need are some bikes and a leader—preferably a black."

The idea was exciting. But where would the church get the money for bikes? They had just hired Ron Cook to help revive the cell groups that had languished after the first sputtering efforts to have them on Sunday afternoon. Where would they get a black and the money to pay him?

The discussion that followed Davenport's talk ended without any definite plans being laid. "We'll pray about it and keep our eyes open," was all Bill could say.

There was still a lot of food left over from the banquet of the night before. They decided Bill and Chuck should take it to the 18th District station where many officers had been on duty since Friday. "Gee, thanks a million," the district's director of community relations said.

"It'll sure taste better than C-rations." But another man in blue was not so appreciative. "Why didn't you bring more meat?" he groused.

By midweek the neighborhood had returned to an uneasy norm. Workers had replaced broken glass in show windows, and grocery store shelves had been restocked. But the burned, black hulks of many buildings remained as a stark reminder of what had happened.

The coffeehouse in the Fellowship Hall resumed on Friday night. The student staffers could sense the hostility of the few blacks who came. Later in the evening and again on Saturday night fights sprang up outside.

Wheaton friends were warning the Leslies not to go through with their plans to move. "Can't you break the lease?" they begged.

Adrienne was apprehensive. "If it were just us, Bill, I wouldn't worry. But we have three children. What if something happens to them?" Bill tried to assure her that things were calming down.

Early in May a group of young blacks stopped to see Bill in the church office. They lived in apartments about a block down LaSalle Street and were students at the University of Illinois Circle Campus on the west side. "We heard you've leased a house on Crilly Court and are moving your family down, Reverend," the spokesman said. Then, unrolling a map, he pointed to shaded areas. "Here is where our people are going to burn," he explained. "The block you're planning to move into is included, but because we like what you are doing for the kids, we came to warn you. Keep your family in the suburbs where it's safe."

Bill tried not to show the clammy fear he felt in the pit of his stomach. "I appreciate the information, but this isn't the way to help. Burning is a cop-out, not a solution."

"Well, we're going to do it anyway," the leader declared. "We hope you'll take our advice and keep your family where they'll be safe."

Bill was shaking his head. "This won't keep us away. We're moving down to help more people. If you burn us and other people out, the responsibility will be yours. I think you ought to reconsider the implications of your actions before striking a single match."

When Bill went home that evening, he told Adrienne, "A bunch of students called on me and predicted more trouble in the neighborhood. But I think, at least I hope, they were just talking."

Bill couldn't bring himself to tell her the details of their threat. He worried, prayed, argued with himself, felt pangs of guilt, and slept very little during the next two weeks.

Nor did he tell Adrienne that their insurance company refused to cover their furniture at the new location.

Moving On

7

Moving On

LEAVING HER LOVELY HOUSE IN WHEATON was traumatic for Adrienne. They still owned the house and were renting it out. But she had the feeling they wouldn't be coming back. As Bill backed the Chevy out of the driveway, she couldn't hold back the sobs.

The tears stopped before they were on the expressway. By the time they were twisting into two-block long Crilly Court, she was actually looking forward to beginning a new chapter in life.

The first morning Adrienne stood at her kitchen window, she saw the colorfully dressed career women from the apartments in back leaving for work. It was like a fashion parade from the display window at Marshall Field or Saks on Fifth Avenue.

The children were up early in anticipation of new adventures, and the family enjoyed breakfast together since Bill did not have to leave before daylight for school.

After breakfast the girls asked if they could ride their bikes. "I don't see why not," Bill said. "Just don't go off our little street." A moment later they came running back. "Our bikes are gone from under the back porch!" reported Lisa. "Somebody took them."

Bill went to the police station and reported the theft. But the desk sergeant gave little assurance the bikes would be found. "Keep 'em in the house from now on," he advised.

Bill returned home to help with the unpacking, then in the afternoon went to do a chore at the church. Adrienne kept busy.

She was putting away a stack of dishes when she heard male voices downstairs and froze. Who was in the house? Her heart pounded apprehensively as she tiptoed to the stairs and peered along the basement hall. There was little Andy talking animatedly with four enormous black men. "Mommy," he called gaily. "Come meet my new friends. They were passing by and I invited them in." All the fears of suburbia gripped her as she tried to remain calm. "I'm afraid we aren't ready for company yet," she said, trying not to offend. "Andy, would you walk your friends back to the door?" Much to Adrienne's relief they left quietly. Then she gave instructions to Andy and the girls that they were never, never under any circumstances to let anyone in the house they didn't know.

But she did want the children to enjoy a full life in the new neighborhood. It offered much to see and do for summer fun. The beach was only a short walk away. The downtown Loop was just minutes by bus. The intriguing shops in Old Town were a few blocks south and Lincoln Park was a block to the east, bordering the beach. Here the children could take free art, ballet, and music lessons, and in the winter go ice skating. Here also was the famous Lincoln Park Zoo, which included a barnyard full of farm animals. The girls squealed with delight and could hardly decide what they wanted to do first.

Adrienne suggested they take ballet. In the daytime it didn't seem dangerous to walk across busy Clark Street as long as they obeyed the traffic light and went with two neighbor girls. But Adrienne quickly learned it wasn't that simple. One afternoon about 5:00 the girls were leaving the building where they had their lessons when a man approached and dropped his pants. "Here comes our mother!" was all that Laurel could think to say, although Adrienne was at home. The man started running but wasn't fast enough for the police officer whom the girls attracted by their yells.

Adrienne was still nervous over the experience when Bill came home. He assured her that it wasn't her fault, that it probably wouldn't happen again, and that if the girls were threatened with danger, police were close by. It would be best, he agreed, never to let the children be out by themselves after dark.

But there would be other close calls. One Thursday a Jewish friend invited seven-year-old Lisa to a birthday party. Bill was out of town for a speaking engagement, and Lisa was begging her mother to let her ride the bus to her friend's apartment house on Sheridan Road.

Adrienne called the friend's mother. "Let her come on," she said. "The bus stops right in front of our building. Call me just before you put her on the bus and I'll meet her when she gets off. When she's ready to come home, I'll call you and you can meet her at your stop." This seemed sensible and Adrienne told Lisa she could go.

About 6:30 that evening the friend's mother called. "She's on the bus and will be there in a few minutes." Adrienne walked over to the stop on Clark Street just a block away and waited. Twenty minutes passed and no bus. Thirty minutes. She flagged down a passing police car and asked the officer why the bus wasn't running.

"Don't you know, lady, we're expecting trouble with the Yippies in the park tonight. That bus took another route after 5:30."

Adrienne was frantic. Lisa wouldn't know how to get home. "What can I do?" she asked.

"Get in and we'll take you down to the station and you can file a lost child report," he said calmly.

The 18th District station was full of police officers, many in plain clothes. They were preparing for a riot. Adrienne made the report, and the dispatcher broadcast a description of Lisa on the police network.

Suddenly Adrienne had the urge to call home. The desk sergeant dialed for her. "Line's busy," he said.

Desperate, Adrienne begged, "Can't you cut in? Something tells me I must talk—right now. Please."

"Aw, lady, don't get upset. We already have a tap on the line. I can get your phone." He pushed some buttons and listened. "They're talking about your daughter!"

Adrienne grabbed the phone and heard one of her neighbors talking to Laurel. The neighbor had been having coffee with a police officer. The volume on his car radio had been turned up, permitting them to hear a report that a little lost girl fitting Lisa's description was at the First District station on the south side of the Loop.

Adrienne sped to the other station in a taxi and ran inside. There was Lisa, the only white person in the entire room, holding a balloon in one hand and a sucker in the other with tears running down her face. Adrienne ran and hugged her, then called to the desk sergeant. "Where is the officer who brought her in? I want to thank him."

He took her to a Sergeant Smith. As Adrienne took his hand, a cloud of tears burst. "Oh, thank you. Thank you," she sobbed.

"Just doing my job, mother," the sergeant said. "The bus driver realized what had happened when he saw her still on the bus at the end of the route. He brought her to me. Just doing my job."

"Give me the driver's name," Adrienne asked. "I want to thank him, too."

"Sure, it's on the paper at the desk."

Back at home, Adrienne called the driver to express her gratefulness. Hearing his soft drawl, she said, "Are you black, too?"

"Yes, ma'am, that's the way God made me."

Adrienne hung up quietly, thinking how good it would be to tell some prejudiced friends about the experience.

Bill still had not told Adrienne the details of the radicals' threat. There was no need, he felt, to alarm her. He didn't think they would carry it out, but he couldn't be sure. He kept his antennae up for neighborhood rumors.

Meanwhile, he was glad to see Adrienne involved in preparing for the next banquet. Because so many had been unable to attend the spring fete in Wheaton, Elm-LaSalle had planned another dinner at the church for Saturday night, June 8.

Adrienne had been saving a collection of miniature kerosene lamps which she had found in a Sav-O-Rama variety store in Wheaton for 29¢ each. The little pseudo-stained glass novelties were imports from Hong Kong. She felt they would add a touch of the exotic. Guests could take them home as a token of the occasion.

The banquet programs came from the leftover stock of a Christian printer. They were purposefully left blank and a toothpick and three tiny vials of paint added to each place setting. While waiting to be served, each person could create his own cover design. Then above the tables, Adrienne and her committee hung butterfly mobiles made of colored tissue paper and reeds.

It helped ease Bill's anxiety to know that Adrienne was conveniently close and on the team as she had been at Pekin. Her nearness seemed to add stability to the entire church. Everyone was reassured that Bill wasn't planning to leave soon.

The banquet was planned to bring together about 30 neighborhood black youths and some prospective white establishment donors. Among the latter were a social-register couple living at the nearby, swank Ambassador Hotel. He was an investment banker, and she belonged to the wealthy Vanderbilt family. Bill and Adrienne had been cultivating their friendship. Also present were Kenneth Taylor, then working on the books of his later-to-be-named *Living Bible*, his wife Margaret, plus several other visitors from the suburbs.

The speaker was John Mosiman, an artist from the staff of missionary radio station HCJB in Ecuador—thus the art motif. But the mood was subdued.

Just two days before, Senator Robert Kennedy had been murdered in Los Angeles. Coming only two months after the death of Martin Luther King, this second assassination had plunged the country into deep introspection.

To make the situation worse, the neighborhood blacks acted rudely, shoving in front of the whites and taking double portions of food. They took so much that at least 30 whites got no food at all.

Although seating was not reserved, the blacks sat in a section by themselves, talking and laughing loudly. When the speaker was introduced, they kept talking. Bill could not condone their behavior, but he sensed the reason. They were resentful of the well-dressed whites who had invaded their turf and now outnumbered them.

Suddenly some chairs scraped. To Bill and Adrienne's dismay, the social-register couple were leaving. The Leslies never saw them again, nor did they ever visit the church. Finally the speaker exhausted his patience and bluntly asked the noisemakers to be quiet. At this point, Harold Brown—the one who had jumped Chuck in a dispute over a pool game—jumped up and yelled to Bill, "Pastor, get these honkies out of here."

The speaker gave up and sat down. Bill was able to recover a semblance of order. There was no violence. But the blacks left smirking and smiling, and the whites departed in gloom.

"We'd have been better off not having it," Bill said to Adrienne in exhaustion and disappointment. "None of the visitors will want to help the youth programs after this."

He was wrong. Kenneth and Margaret Taylor sent a check for $50 with a note promising to continue giving on a regular basis. It was one of the most cheering gifts ever received.

June passed into July. The threat of burning faded, giving Bill immense relief. His laugh seemed merrier, his steps lighter. Another reason was the renewed closeness with Adrienne. They were running on the same track.

They kept in touch with old friends from Wheaton College. One day, Dr. Jaymes Morgan, a former classmate who had been in their wedding, stopped by. "How are things at Fuller?" Bill asked, referring to the seminary at which Morgan was now teaching. "I'm having a ball teaching social ethics," Morgan replied, "although that isn't my title. Many of our supporters still see liberal when they hear 'social ethics.' But I'm here to see what Elm-LaSalle is doing. I've been nearing some stories."

Bill grinned as he began telling the visitor about the church's traumas and triumphs. "Hey, that's great," Morgan kept saying. "Just great. Your church is a pioneer. I can't wait to tell my students."

Around Chicago, verbal conflicts over race and other social issues were heating up between church leaders. Blacks and liberal Protestants had Evangelicals on the defensive.

Item: Rev. C. T. Vivian, a black civil rights leader, confronted Dr. Kenneth Kantzer, Dean of Trinity Evangelical Divinity School, on the University of Chicago's Radio Round Table. Subject: racism in churches. Vivian charged that conservative churches exhibited racial hatred. Kantzer vigorously denied this and went on to cite Wheaton as an example of progress. Wheaton, he said, had been one of the first towns in the Midwest to pass an open-housing law.

Two months later, David Mains challenged the pastors of the Evangelical Free Church of America, Trinity's denominational sponsor. At their annual conference, Mains called on the pastors to sign a statement saying people of any race would be welcome in their churches if the people wished to be helpful. The majority were unwilling.

By this time key legislative goals of the civil rights movement had been reached and blacks were looking beyond integration. "Black Power"—a term that scared misinformed whites—was in vogue. But it made sense to Bill Leslie and the thin line of workers at Elm-LaSalle. Blacks, they felt, needed to build their own power bases in government, commerce, schools, housing, and other areas in which whites had so long held control. They had to become masters of their own destiny.

It was not always easy, however, to maintain this position in view of what was happening at the coffeehouse. Every Friday and Saturday night irresponsible blacks, high on cheap wine, taunted the white hippies and pinched and propositioned the white Wheaton girls who served on the staff. "You're all damn hypocrites," they would say. "You come downtown on weekends and during the summer, then you go back to your white colleges in the fall. We have to stay here all year round." Such harangues could be tolerated, but the leering, pinching, and obscene talk to the girls could not. Bill had to tell the girls to stay in Wheaton.

One night at a committee meeting, called in an effort to keep the coffeehouse open, Harold Brown's brother Harry stood on a bench and began denouncing white churches. "You ain't done a damn thing for this community," he yelled. "Put your white Jesus back in your bag and get the hell out."

Bill took young Brown by the arm. "Look, your behavior isn't measuring up to our expectations. You'll have to leave." In spite of his tirades, Brown respected Bill and left. But others who were evicted remained outside to pick fights with behaving guests as they left.

103

The fights attracted passing police, and Bill had to go to the station and plead for the release of troublemakers. Finally, after the second trip to the station house one night, even he and Chuck Hogren found that their patience was exhausted. Reluctantly, they recommended in July, 1968, that The Extension be closed.

Fortunately, this sad event had been anticipated. Back in March the church had opened another coffeehouse across LaSalle Street in safer territory. The "Yellow House" was an antiquated frame bungalow that stood next to the old brick mansion used two years before for the Saturday night sing-a-longs. Both houses were owned by the same family, who had tagged the "Yellow House" for demolition. The family agreed that the church could use it until the wreckers came.

Two dating couples—Don Denton and Beth Beckon, and Rod Berg and Gina Jemison—painted the living and dining room floors black and covered the ceiling with yellow streamers. Friday and Saturday nights, it was a coffeehouse. Weekdays, it was a distribution center for used clothing donated by suburban churches. Don, a Vietnam veteran, also lived in the house.

As chief bouncer, Don made certain rules: No disturbances, no molesting of girls, and no prowling in the kitchen. One rainy night in August, his mettle was firmly tested.

About 35 people were inside, and half of them seemed to be violating the rules. Don singled out a tall ex-marine as the chief instigator. Though several inches shorter, he grabbed the troublemaker and pushed him against the wall. Then standing back suddenly and putting his hands on his hips like an angry drill instructor, Don said firmly, "Leave, or I'll throw you out." The disturber departed peacefully and the rest calmed down.

Deciding how far to go in helping penniless youth was harder. Rod Berg was a soft touch. Don Denton knew human nature better than the gentle Swede and kept an eye out for addicts looking for a handout to feed their habit and other con-artists. Several times he had to remind Rod, "They're ripping you off, man." And Rod would reply, "Maybe so, but I've got to listen."

By this time Old Town had become a mecca for runaway teenagers.

Bill was getting calls from distraught parents, asking if he had seen their children. He always had to answer no. Thousands of flower children carried backpacks and hoofed along the streets of Old Town in sandals or barefoot. Finding a particular youth was about as likely as scooping a marble from Lake Michigan.

What Elm-LaSallers did do was join with others and rent an office and a phone—the digits spelled KOOLAID—that runaways could call. Callers and runaways dropping in at the church or coffeehouse were usually sent to a local agency called "The Looking Glass." The agency would then call and say, "Your son (or daughter) is here. May we have permission to keep him tonight?" That was essential because persons harboring underaged runaways without explicit parental permission could be arrested for contributing to their delinquency.

Since some persons stood ready to take advantage of stray youth, the police enforced that law vigorously. Still, several Elm-LaSalle singles and couples took a chance on kids who had nowhere else to stay and whose parents could not be reached. Only Beth, a thin, diminutive 19-year-old who looked 13, was ever jailed.

Beth took in a 17-year-old Italian girl who spoke only about 30 words of English. Rosa was obviously the daughter of Italian aliens or recent immigrants, but whenever Beth asked about her parents, she would shake her head and burst into tears.

A few evenings later the police pushed into Beth's apartment and announced she was under arrest. They took her in a squad car to the police station where she was booked, fingerprinted, and put in a cell. Rosa's father, who had earlier deserted his family, had somehow discovered where she was staying and had pressed charges.

The police allowed Beth to call Don. Within minutes, he, Bill, Chuck, and several others arrived to make bail.

Chuck appeared as her defense attorney at the trial. When he finished, the judge looked across at the frail, frightened girl, who looked younger than the runaway she had been charged with harboring. "It's preposterous of me to convict this girl. She never should have been arrested."

After only six months of operation, the Yellow House met the same fate as The Extension. One evening a crowd of black radicals stormed in with clubs. Seeing that he was outnumbered, Don Denton raced out the back door and left the invaders to prowl through the stock of used clothing. Shortly after this experience, financial difficulties forced the operation to be shut down.

Elm-LaSalle was still just scraping by financially, although the church building was usually full for Sunday worship services. The congregation lacked solid wage earners.

Moody Church had problems, too. As families left for the suburbs, it was generally the lower-salaried people who stayed. The enormous building required considerable maintenance. The board at the time represented the more conservative faction of the church and no doubt did not represent the congregation as a whole. Add to this the fact that the board made almost all the decisions, while many in the congregation sided with Elm-LaSalle. When Elm-LaSalle asked for congregational independence, a committee came to Bill with a proposal.

"There's no need to have two churches so close together," they said. "Why not close up Elm-LaSalle and bring your young people to the mother church? This is a time for Evangelicals to come together. We have plenty of room." The suggestion took Bill by surprise. But he continued to listen.

"We haven't always agreed with your ideas, Bill, but we'd still like you back on the staff as youth minister. Maybe we could sell the building for $90,000 and use the money to renovate our building."

"Well, I couldn't make that decision," Bill said. "I'll ask our people and see what they think."

The following Sunday Bill told Elm-LaSallers what the committee had said. He asked for those who would be willing to attend Moody Church to raise their hands. Only three of about 300 did. Afterward, Chuck Hogren and another member told Bill why they were negative. "There are no young people on the Moody Church board. Our views wouldn't be heard."

Bill reported back to the Moody committee that the merger was not possible.

From the standpoint of the condition of Elm-LaSalle's building, the idea was tempting. Without some basic repairs, the old church would soon fall apart. Paint was peeling. Several windows were broken. Stair banisters were loose. Jagged pew edges tore women's hose. Plaster fell from the high ceiling when the organ hit a high note.

Elm-LaSalle was still hoping to purchase the building. But the Moody Church board had become tired of waiting and decided to put it on the market.

Bill saw the handwriting on the wall. Elm-LaSalle had to expand its corps of adult leaders and financial supporters if it was ever to buy the building or find facilities elsewhere. But where would they find suburban people willing to come into the city?

Bill had an idea which seemed God-given. Lay members in suburban churches were being asked to volunteer for short-term assignments in foreign countries. Why not issue such a challenge to serve in the city?

Quickly, enthusiastically, Bill typed a letter outlining the opportunities for service, suggesting that married couples consider committing a year of Sundays and tithes. Their children, he pointed out, could remain active in the weekday organizations of their home church. He mailed copies of the letter to 30 pastors whom he thought might present the idea to their congregations. Not one bothered to reply. Other copies went to lay acquaintances in the Wheaton area. One Wheaton college faculty member, Alice Naumoff, had been coming for a couple of years. She had brought Anne Martin, a Wheaton grad who was a career social worker. Was it too much to hope that other faculty members and graduates of the college might see the city as their mission field?

The issue was now Vietnam. The war was dividing the country and even causing fierce arguments among Evangelicals over the morality of American intervention. Elm-LaSalle's youngish congregation included both enlisted service personnel stationed in the Chicago area and draft resisters. The church board considered it a matter of individual conscience, declaring that the church would pray for those going to war while giving support to conscientious objectors.

To establish official C.O. status and avoid legal penalties, an objector's church had to have a pacifistic background. At a federal hearing for Elm-LaSalle's Jim Albertson, a student at the Art Institute, a government official reported on the history of Moody Church. "The founder, Dwight L. Moody, was a pacifist during the Civil War," he stated. He recommended that Albertson be classified C.O.

While peace between the two sides reigned in Elm-LaSalle, massive campus unrest had reached all the way to the White House. Lyndon Johnson had announced he would not run again. Now the radical leaders of the anti-war movement had been gearing up for the Democratic National Convention in Chicago the last week of August. Mayor Daley had declared, "No one is going to take over the streets." To reinforce that pledge he decreed that the city's entire 12,000-member police force would go on 12-hour shifts, and National Guard and regular army reinforcements would be requested.

The serious radicals were concentrating on the convention headquarters. The ludicrous Yippies announced plans for a Festival of Life in Lincoln Park during which they would "nominate" a pig named Pigasus for president. The police were not amused and hauled the pig off to the Humane Society.

The threat of a confrontation between the taunting Yippies and the police kept building. The Yippies were sleeping in Lincoln Park without a permit, and the police were trying to get them out. Patrol cars ringed the park while helicopters fluttered overhead day and night.

Sunday, August 25, was a low day at the church. With most of the students still on summer vacations, only about 40 worshipers came for morning services. Bill was winding up his sermon when a middle-aged couple entered and took seats in a back pew. He could hardly wait to greet his old friends from Wheaton College, Dr. Arthur and Ruth Volle.

"Sorry we're late," Arthur apologized. "We thought your services were at 11:00." Then he added with a smile, "we got your letter and have come to offer a year of our lives."

Late Sunday night the police went into Lincoln Park after the Yippies with Mace, tear gas, and riot sticks. Over 3,500 boys and girls came pouring out, many of them only high school kids who had come in from the suburbs for the excitement.

The Leslies' close friends, David and Karen Mains, had a bird's-eye view from the windows of their third-floor Georgian Court apartment that looked out to the park. They watched in horror as hundreds raced into the U-shaped courtyard, pursued by blue-helmeted police swinging riot sticks. Above the frantic ringing of their buzzer, they could hear the sickening crunch of wood against skulls.

David ran to the door and pushed the button that released the downstairs lock while Karen shouted out the window, "Come up through here!" Instantly, the stairs were alive with pounding feet. Then the horde was running through the apartment, out the back way, and down the fire escape to Crilly Court. One frightened boy dove under their bed, but David pulled him out and told him to move on.

The Leslies, watching from their upstairs window, saw figures running along the dark street. Suddenly powerful floodlights turned the street into day and the fleeing Yippies dived under cars. Police swarmed in after them with Mace and tear gas, dragged them out, and pounded heads, while the young daredevils fought vigorously to get away. It was a true nightmare in living color.

Day and night throughout the convention week the police pursued protestors around the downtown area. The biggest battle came on Thursday night in Grant Park across Michigan Avenue from the Hilton Hotel. The anti-war mob massed in the park, cursing and hurling bags of human excrement at the police. Enraged, the police finally moved in, swinging their clubs, going after anti-war people along with reporters and broadcasters in the crowd. The bloody melee, shown on television, stirred bitter disputes across the country over who was to blame, the police or the activists. Reporters and anti-war forces called the week's events a police riot and specifically blamed Mayor Daley. Law-and-order advocates defended Daley and said his police saved the peace by their brave and courageous enforcement.

Most Elm-LaSalle people felt the police were unnecessarily brutal. Bill and Ron Cook saw two police officers jump from their car on LaSalle Street and club a defenseless long-haired youth and his girl friend to the ground. Mike Royko, the cryptic, satirical columnist of the *Chicago Daily News*, wrote that he had walked in the worst neighborhoods of Chicago all his life, "but the only time I've run to save my hide was when a group of Chicago police were after me."

Monday was Labor Day, and the Leslies relaxed and tried to look ahead. One cloud on the horizon would not go away. It was the dread of sending Laurel and Lisa to public school on Wednesday.

Then on Tuesday the principal of the private Harris School called. "I've been thinking about your girls all summer," he told Adrienne. "They're so bright that we just can't allow them to attend public school. We're going to somehow make room for them."

It seemed to Adrienne that her heart was pounding out the words, "Thank God, thank God, thank God."

"And I'm sure that because of your husband's limited income they'll qualify for scholarships," he added.

"Short Terms" in the City

8

"Short Terms" in the City

ARTHUR VOLLE, a tall, soft-spoken Iowan, held a doctorate from Northwestern. He had come to Wheaton College as a vocational counselor in 1946, later served as dean, and had recently returned to full-time counseling duties. He and Mrs. Volle had been discussing the crisis of the cities with friends at the College Church in Wheaton. They decided that since their children were grown they should "look for something to do." Then Bill's letter came.

They were quickly put to work at Elm-LaSalle. Ruth Volle was charged with securing volunteers to serve refreshments at the after-worship Fellowship Hour. Arthur was tabbed to start a "street academy" for helping high school dropouts qualify for diplomas.

A consortium of west-side churches was already doing this through the Christian Action Ministry (CAM). Early in September Bill, Chuck, and Arthur looked over the CAM operation. The procedure was to give applicants diagnostic tests to determine their basic knowledge levels, then assign them to individual counselors for developmental guidance. "Our only difficulty," the CAM director observed, "is that we have more applicants than counselors."

When the word got out at Elm-LaSalle, three young blacks applied immediately. Arthur gave them tests and scheduled weekly sessions with three volunteer counselors: Bob Watson, a recent law school graduate; Anita Smith, an inner-city teacher; and Betsy Glanville, a social worker.

The following Sunday, Arthur stopped at the curb to let Ruth out in front of the church and saw his name on the outside bulletin board. It read:

William H. Leslie, Pastor

Ronald Cook, Assistant Pastor

Arthur H. Volle, Ph.D., Director of Counseling

Every Thursday evening he made the 60-mile round trip into the city to work with Charles Taylor (the brother of Harold), his 18-year-old counselee. One Thursday night Charles failed to show up. Arthur saw him the next Sunday and asked what had happened. "Oh, I just forgot, Doc," he said with a hangdog look. "I'll be there next Thursday."

"Better call the church before you come," Bill advised Arthur. "Time isn't as important to these fellows as it is to you."

Dr. Don and Betty Boardman came a few weeks after the Volles in response to Bill's letter. A geology professor at Wheaton, Don became a valuable resource person for students having intellectual problems about their faith. Betty edited the church newspaper, *Guidelines*.

Lois Ottaway, news director of the college, was next. Raised on a Kansas farm, she had been "shaken to the core" by the riots following Martin Luther King's death, then "shocked" by the lack of response from Wheaton churches. One day her secretary said, "Hey, I've been going to this neat church downtown that has real social concern. Why don't you try it?" She did and became the church's volunteer publicist. She later helped in the PACE (Programmed Activities for Correctional Education) program at the Cook County Jail and gave inmates vocational training one night a week.

With the Volles, the Boardmans, and Lois Ottaway, Elm-LaSalle was taking on a new establishment look. More volunteers were yet to come.

114

Don and Madelyn Powell were already living in the city. Don had been a Fulbright professor of engineering in Turkey and was now a partner in a business specializing in research and testing of automotive equipment. He was a graduate of Ohio State, and "Maddy" had attended Moody Bible Institute.

The Powells were long-time members of Moody Church. Don had served on the Moody Church board since 1955 and was one of Elm-LaSalle's strongest supporters. Maddy had been a research assistant for George Sweeting.

Don and Maddy did not make the change lightly. The civil rights revolution had forced them to reassess their life-styles and goals. First, they made a commitment to remain in their racially changing south-shore neighborhood, even though their house had been burglarized twice and most white residents were fleeing. As the neighborhood changed from a majority of white to a majority of black, they read books by black writers, the *Report of the National Advisory Commission on Civil Disorders*, and other materials on urban crime and violence. They also subscribed to periodicals with different viewpoints from the conservative ones they had been reading.

They joined a discussion group called "Conversations on the City," composed of Evangelicals concerned about applying Biblical principles to urban problems. After Martin Luther King's assassination, they began visiting new black neighbors and learned how keenly they mourned the civil rights leader's death and how they lived in fear of violence. They noticed that their friends kept their shades drawn even during the day because they didn't want passersby to know they were black.

Don had long been interested in student ministries and was a national board member of Inter-Varsity Christian Fellowship. (He would become chairperson of the IVCF board the following year.) He understood the conflicts among Evangelicals over social issues. As a boy, he had often heard his fundamentalist pastor-father talk about the fundamentalist-modernist split over theology and the Social Gospel.

In the mid-sixties the Powells became convinced Elm-LaSalle was on the right track in calling Evangelicals back to a more balanced ministry. One Sunday evening in 1968 Don accompanied Maddy to Elm-LaSalle where she was to lead a Bible study. Afterward, they overheard Jaymes Morgan from Fuller tell someone, "Be sure you put your affiliations where your convictions are." The Powells decided their convictions lay with the struggling branch church.

These "establishment" Evangelicals who came in the fall of '68 gave Elm-LaSalle a desperately needed boost and a new image of stability.

The Volles and Boardmans pledged only one year in response to Bill's letter. But in the fall of 1969 they said they would stay on indefinitely. A third key suburban couple, Dick and Connie Turner, came at this time in response to the short-term request.

Dick Turner, a Wheaton College grad and a school principal, had first heard about the church from Adrienne when she was teaching art at Franklin Elementary School in Wheaton. When Bill wrote the letter, Adrienne suggested he send the Turners a copy.

At the time Dick was also serving as superintendent of the Wheaton Bible Church's large Sunday school of over 1,000 enrollment. Bill's letter came when the Turners were moving toward more personal involvement in promoting better understanding between blacks and whites.

The year before, Dick had initiated a student exchange with an inner-city black school under the federally funded Wing Spread program. Each school bussed 15 sixth-graders to the other for the experiment in race relations. Dick received only one complaint. "You have no business mixing the races with my tax money," a woman caller railed. "We don't need the city. If Chicago cut itself off from the suburbs, we'd be just as well off." Dick disagreed, saying, "Suburban workers commute into the city every day to earn a living for their families. We're all in this together."

As the exchange continued, Dick and Connie read books on the urban scene and Connie took a course on black studies at Wheaton College.

They tried to make the Wheaton Bible Church more aware. Dick proposed a summer study on church and society. The church board voted it down. One member grumbled, "Why stir up these problems out here?" But the adult Sunday school classes did invite three black Evangelical leaders to talk on different Sundays.

When Bill's letter came, the Turners decided to spend a Sunday in the city before making any commitment. Dick got a fill-in at the Wheaton Bible Church. Connie packed a picnic lunch, and they took along a tape recorder, music cassettes, and two blankets. Their children—Nancy, 16; Susan, 14; and Jim, 11—were excited about the adventure.

They enjoyed the worship service and the Fellowship Hour. Then they drove over to the lake and spread their blankets on a grassy spot beside the Adler Planetarium. Reclining on the blankets, eating, listening to music, and watching the picture-card sailboats drift by turned out to be a delightful experience. About 3:00 they went back to the church and looked in on the afternoon tutoring. It was an inspiration to see such examples of caring.

They enjoyed a snack supper in a downtown restaurant, participated in the evening forums at the church, then drove home. The family vote was unanimous in favor of giving a year to Elm-LaSalle.

Dick felt, however, that he should finish out his year's term as Sunday school superintendent for the Bible Church. In the six months intervening they read everything available on black culture and the city, and Dick and Connie brushed up on teaching methods. None of this really prepared them for experiences to come.

Connie accepted a Sunday school class of fifth and sixth graders. Trying to disguise her nervousness, the tall, blond, suburban woman walked across the crowded fellowship hall and introduced herself to seven noisy black girls and one white—Laurel Leslie—grouped around a table. She spoke loudly because of the hubbub in the large room. A half-dozen other classes, separated only by the portable screens, were already in progress.

As soon as the girls told her their names, she proposed an activity. Immediately, Josie, a large black girl as tall as Connie, retorted, "Naw, let's do something else." From this point Josie took over. Nothing Connie said agreed with her. Each time she felt like it, she trooped off to the washroom with the other blacks following. When 11-year-old Jim Turner brought juice and cookies, Josie jumped up and grabbed the cookie platter. "You get two, and you were bad, so you get one," she said, starting around the table. Connie could only look on helplessly.

The two teenage Turners were helping with younger children and having no problems. But Dick was having his troubles with seven black boys about the same ages as Connie's girls. At the Wheaton Bible Church he had trained the teachers. Here the boys were making him look like a fool. Nothing seemed to command their interest. In ten minutes he was out of ideas and frantically trying to restore order. The boys ignored him, jumping around the table, and poking and picking at one another in wild abandon. It was as if he wasn't there.

Dick and Connie were determined to build friendship and rapport with their students. "Ask your parents if you can spend next Saturday afternoon with us in Wheaton," they invited. "We'll have a picnic, go swimming, play ball, and have a lot of fun."

At first only the boys were allowed to go. Parents were afraid their daughters would be abused in the suburbs. Not wanting to cause problems with their neighbors, the Turners put down some ground rules for the kids: "Stay in our yard. If the ball bounces into a neighbor's yard, let us go after it. And be careful not to bump parked cars when you're riding bikes."

The black children drew the Turners into a world they had never known in their small-town rearing or in Wheaton. They found that these fifth- and sixth-graders were behind suburban children in academic learning but far ahead in their awareness of gut-level issues of city life.

One fatherless boy, Mike, could barely read. But he lived next door to a warlock from a Satanist church and knew more about the occult than most college students. Dick took Mike under his wing, tutored him in reading, and brought him to Wheaton for Christmas. Mike's facade of toughness melted away.

After a few months the girls obtained permission to visit the Turners. Dick and Connie took them to their neighborhood pool. "Can

everybody swim?'' Connie asked. ''Yeah, yeah!'' Josie chortled and
jumped in. They pulled her out half-drowned.

Dick mentioned this to Bill and asked, ''Why do they say they can
do something when they can't?''

''They're trying to cover up insecurities. When they're out in
Wheaton, they're off their turf and fearful of being laughed at or put
down. They really lack self-confidence. What they need most is
affirming love. We who were raised in nice, comfortable secure
homes by two parents have a hard time understanding this need. They
need to be constantly affirmed, commended, encouraged, and helped
to build a good self-image.''

This soon became obvious to the Turners. When Connie passed out
magazine cutouts of children and asked her girls to pick their prefer-
ences, almost invariably they selected whites before blacks. Both she
and Dick tried reading them short, simple biographies of famous
blacks. Still, they did not seem to think black was beautiful.

Connie remained uptight and ill at ease. She was afraid of saying
something that would lower the little self-esteem that had been built
up. Fortunately, this tension was snapped one day in Sunday school.

''Miz Turner,'' big Josie asked. ''Is my face black?'' Connie
thought she was trying to overcome a color complex. She looked at her
a long time, then said, ''Josie, I really think it's dark brown.''

''Oh, I don't mean that,'' Josie said. ''I mean, is it dirty?''

''This is silly,'' Connie decided. ''So what if I say something
wrong. I'm just going to be myself.'' After that the class time and
conversations with the girls went much better.

The Turners were now spending all day Sunday downtown. After
church they made an adventure out of eating at a different ethnic
restaurant each Sunday. At three o'clock they went back to the church
to help in tutoring, then remained for the evening forums.

Across the country there was growing Evangelical interest in social
ministries. *Eternity* magazine's ''Book of the Year'' for 1968 was *The
Social Conscience of the Evangelical* by Sherwood Wirt, editor of
Billy Graham's *Decision* magazine. The previous year not a single
book on social concern had made *Eternity*'s top 25. In 1969 the

National Association of Evangelicals held its first conference on the inner city. Closer to home, George Sweeting led Moody Church to open a day-care center for children of working mothers on the near-north side.

But the racial fears and conflicts were still far from settled. The hackles of many Evangelical leaders were up against black demands for restitution. In the spring of 1969, James Forman issued his famous "Manifesto" calling for white churches and synagogues to pay blacks $500 million. This, along with some black radicals advocating guerrilla warfare, scared whites.

White Evangelical institutions continued to be caught in the middle between pragmatists who feared loss of donor support and activists who wanted change at whatever cost.

In Chicago, for example, the Timothy Christian School, operated by the Christian Reformed Church (CRC), was caught in the crossfire. The trustees of the school ordered that blacks be denied admittance. The policy provoked immediate protests. Four of the eleven teachers resigned, and students from the CRC's Calvin College came from Michigan to picket. The trustees then ordered the school closed.

The waters were also troubled at Moody Bible Institute. Melvin Warren, a black graduating senior and a former assistant pastor at Circle Church, released a lengthy complaint against school racism to the press. He claimed the school had long forbade interracial dating and assigned dormitory rooms on the basis of color. MBI's public relations director replied that the dating policy was no longer in effect and denied discrimination in room assignments. Nevertheless, Warren and some friends picketed briefly in protest outside the school's entrance on LaSalle Street.

Several students and alumni who attended Elm-LaSalle urged the MBI administration to help the students become more effective in ministering to the black community. One was Elm-LaSalle's Carol Stine, a white senior, who joined an alumnus of the '68 class in writing an open letter to the school newspaper (May 24, 1969). They felt,

> . . . an addition to the faculty would be helpful for instruction on the Black man—his thinking, his life, his problems, etc. In addition,

Personal Evangelism classes could emphasize a portion on "Negro Evangelism." The Home Missions course, now in existence, could include a larger section on the Negro culture within Protestantism. Selected Negro speakers in chapel could acquaint the student body with the Black community in depth. In short, permit us to be intelligent, effective channels for our Lord's use in metropolitan Chicago. We, the students, admit our ignorance. We ask for help.

While MBI was weighing this request and others, Inter-Varsity Christian Fellowship, with encouragement from Elm-LaSalle, opened a new coffeehouse named "Rahab's" in the middle of Old Town. The MBI Practical Work Department gave a stereo speaker system. MBI students served on the staff, one as manager, with other workers coming from Wheaton, Trinity, and North Park colleges. It was billed as a new thrust in inner-city evangelism.

Rahab's seemed an instant success. It was crowded on weekends. Scores of street youth made professions of faith in Christ. Chicago Evangelical publications and pulpits gave glowing endorsements, saying that the Gospel was indeed relevant to the "now generation" and that Christ was the answer to the drug problem.

But all the press agentry sounded hollow when reports spread that three of the student staffers had been drawn into the drug culture. The alarm went off at the institutions and some withdrew support. Rahab's was abruptly closed.

Ten of the original student promoters huddled in an emergency all-day conference in Wisconsin and decided to reopen. All went well until the spring of 1970, when city inspectors ordered the place shut down until a triple sink and a new ventilating system were installed.

Students on the various campuses raised money for the equipment, and Rahab's reopened for the third time in July, 1970, This time the problem was black agitators storming in night after night, pushing their way to the platform, preaching violent revolution. On a Friday night in August a staffer looked out the door and saw the agitators marching toward the coffeehouse in a phalanx. He bolted the door and warned the others to get out. They ran to a van left parked in back and escaped. This marked the end of the Old Town Rahab's, although

Trinity College students later opened up a coffeehouse with the same name further north near Evanston.

The abortive project had at least succeeded in drawing the attention of more Evangelicals to the city. For one thing, it made students in suburban schools more aware of Circle and Elm-LaSalle, where many of Rahab's staffers attended. For another, it encouraged organizations such as Youth for Christ and Young Life, whose involvement in the city was increasing.

Young Life had had a proven ministry in New York City for several years. Now it was seeking to build a staff in Chicago. Young Life's local urban ministries director, George Scheffer, spent many hours with Bill Leslie discussing how young blacks might be reached.

The biggest need was black staffers. Mel Warren was now working with the Reformed Church of America's mission to blacks in the Robert Taylor Homes' housing project on the south side. Circle Church had hired as associate pastor, Clarence Hilliard, a black attending Trinity Seminary. Elm-LaSalle was still looking for a black staff member, with Bill admitting, "I don't know where we'll get the money to pay him."

Young Life had one promising black who had recently been visiting inmates at the Cook County Jail and reportedly had stumbled on a bribery ring among guards distributing cigarettes to prisoners for pay. "I'll fix that," he told friends, and began giving cigarettes away to prisoners himself.

One evening he and his wife parked outside their apartment. As they were walking toward the door, a car drew up and a voice called to him. When he walked back, an arm reached out of the rear window and pulled him against the auto body. At that instant, the driver took off, leaving him hanging in air. As the car roared under a viaduct, the man in the rear seat suddenly shoved him against the viaduct wall. Police found him dead, his skull crushed. His murderers were never caught, but rumors persisted that he had been killed for meddling in affairs at the jail.

The death of the Young Lifer, whom Bill knew well, merited only a few lines in the daily papers. Blacks died violently in Chicago every day. But another tragedy that happened closer to Elm-LaSalle Church made headlines.

Bruce Johnson was pastor of the Armitage Avenue United Methodist Church, only a short walk from the Leslies' house. On Monday, September 29, he and his wife, Eugenia, were found stabbed to death in their north-side apartment. They had been the center of controversy because of their work with the Black Panthers and two Puerto Rican gangs. Some of their church members had left because he had let the Young Lords use a part of the church for their headquarters and a day-care center.

The police had no definitive clues to the identity of the criminals. There was speculation that the Johnsons might have been killed by a drug addict trying to get money for his habit. Or a disgruntled gang member. Or an underworld figure hired by corrupt politicians who the minister had been threatening to expose.

Bill had known the Johnsons only casually, although they had attended Garrett Seminary in the early '60s. Still, coming so soon after the murder of the Young Lifer, their deaths could not help but make him wonder who would be next. The city was so big. The increasing violence, so irrational. The issues, so complex. And Elm-LaSalle was so small, with its future so uncertain.

LaSalle's Pastor Bill Leslie (above) and the members of the church staff . . . "striving to be God's ministering people."

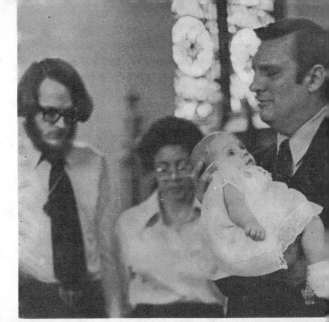

Left:
Adrienne Leslie
and her two oldest
children, Laurel
and Lisa, take
a break between
kitchen chores.

Right:
A moment of
quiet meditation
as Rebecca Ann Berg
is dedicated and
her parents recommit
their own lives.

Below:
New musical sounds
echo from LaSalle's
historic building,
proclaiming the age-old
message of Christ.

Top: Dick and Connie Turner share in an informal fellowship hour.
Bottom: Robert Moore leads in devotions at a senior citizens' Sunday morning breakfa[s]

Above:
Church staff members
at work (left to
right): Earl Laman,
Marlene Pedigo,
Lynette Surbaugh,
Bill Leslie,
Beverly Barr,
Dave Mack.

Right:
Fellowship hour
draws many faces and
hearts together.

Above:
Easter morning
worship . . .
"He is risen!"

Right:
The LaSalle St.
"Lakers" participating
in the Boys' Club
tournament.

Above:
Members of LaSalle
dramatically present
the Story of Esther
to bring the
Bible to life.

Right:
Don and Betty
Boardman share in
fellowship times
with fellow LaSallers.

Chuck Hogren (above)
Director of the Legal
Aid Clinic, and Attorney
Dan Van Ness (right)
consult with clients.

Left:
Earl Laman, Minister
of Counseling at
the Near North
Counseling Center.

Photos by
Richard Ball

Above:
Organist Anita Smith
ministers to the
congregation through
her musical talents.

Left:
One-on-one gives the
LaSalle tutoring program
its impetus—and
its strength.

Top: Proprietor Stan Shank serves customers in his most unusual Logos Bookstore.
Bottom: When learning takes place, sometimes it's almost visible.

Above:
LaSalle's location puts it smack in the life of the city.

Right:
The starkness of the Cabrini-Green housing development, just blocks away.

Charting the Future

9

Charting the Future

The next blow was the decision of the Moody Church board to try to sell the Elm-LaSalle building for $95,000. After the resolution was passed, the chairman of the trustee committee took Bill to lunch and tried to explain why the action had been taken. A majority of board members, he said, honestly felt that Elm-LaSalle had drifted from the fundamentals of the faith. They believed the money from the sale could be put to better use in the Lord's work.

This trustee was a good friend who had contributed money privately to Elm-LaSalle. Bill was not angry at him. But he was exasperated beyond words at the action.

Bill held his anger in until he arrived at home. Then before Adrienne he poured out all his frustration and aggravation. "They'd better not sell the church," he sputtered. "If they do, I'll . . . I'll . . . I'll . . ." Adrienne listened until he finally ran down. All she could think to say was, "Bill, don't do anything you'll regret later."

Ironically, the decision of the Moody Church board to sell the Elm-LaSalle building came during a time when Evangelicals were opening up to new dimensions in ministry. Here and there, respected voices were being heard.

One was Leighton Ford, associate evangelist to Billy Graham. In a major address to the U.S. Congress on Evangelism held in Minneapolis during September, 1969, Ford had declared:

> It is to the shame of the Christian Church that we have been so slow
> to face the demands of the Gospel in the racial revolution of our
> time. With some notable exceptions, we have moved only when we
> have been run over from behind. We have enjoyed, many of us, our
> privileged position at the "white hand of God."
>
> We cannot be worthy of our high calling if we try to keep God in
> some private, undisturbed corner of our lives and ignore the driving
> winds of change. While revolution was raging in Petrograd in 1917,
> the Russian Orthodox Church was in session a few blocks away
> having a hot debate—about what color vestments their priests
> should wear! God help us if we strain at gnats while the camels of
> revolution are marching.

Ford pointed to the "widespread disillusionment, almost disgust,
with the Church" among youth. "The brightest and most sensitive of
our youth too often turn from the Church, accusing us of having as our
theme song, 'I Believe in Yesterday,' and of being irrelevant to the
realities of the 20th century."

The Johnson-Nyquist Company of Los Angeles had produced a film
on the Minneapolis Congress of Evangelism. As a follow-up, they
were looking for a church that blended evangelism and social concern,
preferably an independent Evangelical congregation. David Anderson, the associate producer, talked to Jaymes Morgan at Fuller Seminary.

"Only one in the country fits your requirements," he said. "Elm-
LaSalle Bible Church in Chicago."

Anderson was skeptical. "Bible" churches had a reputation of
opposing anything that smacked of the Social Gospel. "Elm-LaSalle
is the one you want," Morgan reassured him. "I guarantee it."

Anderson called Bill Leslie and explained what he had in mind.
"I'll have to clear it with our staff," Bill said.

The staff was opposed. What Elm-LaSalle was doing had not been
perfected, they argued. Marj Branch was the most adamant against it:
"Blacks in this community are sick of being studied." She explained
that after the 1968 riots, a horde of graduate students and social
scientists had poured into the neighborhood from the University of

Chicago and other academic shrines. Practically every resident of Cabrini-Green had been interviewed. "They've all left now and the people are bitter. They say the researchers earned money and degrees from them."

Bill phoned Anderson about the staff's feelings. "We understand your reservations," the Californian countered. "But you guys have a responsibility to the rest of the body of Christ."

Bill went back to the staff. They conceded Anderson's point. But they would have to hold veto power over the contents.

Anderson and his crew came for seven days. They trailed Bill around in the neighborhood, shooting scenes and recording Bill's narration about what he felt. They filmed church activities and taped comments from Bill, Omer Reese, Bill Bentley (a black Evangelical pastor in Chicago), and a few others. Bill Leslie and the Elm-LaSalle staff made a few cuts and were satisfied with "The Heart Cannot Run."

Now the film company needed a distributor. Billy Zeoli, president of Gospel Films, was an old friend from Bill's Wheaton days. His company would make 150 prints and distribute the film on condition that he be allowed to edit.

Zeoli told the film producer that statements by Bill Bentley about white racism and the failures of white Evangelicals would "not play in Iowa." He suggested that it was better to say a little and get an audience than to communicate nothing at all. "Let God use somebody else to say the rest," he added.

Bill and the Elm-LaSalle staff reluctantly agreed to the cuts. After all, Johnson-Nyquist and Gospel Films were footing the bill.

The film drew plaudits for Elm-LaSalle from some Evangelical leaders. It gave the church an air of respectability. Elm-LaSalle was named "One of Tomorrow's Churches Today" by *Action* magazine, the official organ of the National Association of Evangelicals. But among rank and file Evangelicals the film was no box-office hit.

There was one complaint. A member of the Moody Church board felt the mother church should have been mentioned. "We didn't think you'd want to be associated with us," was Bill's reply.

Some six months after the film was released, agreement was reached with Moody Church for Elm-LaSalle to become an independent congregation and legal entity. Elm-LaSalle could continue to use the building until it was sold.

In the incorporation Elm-LaSalle Bible Church became simply LaSalle Street Church. "Elm" was not a major street. "Bible" had linked the church to a fundamentalist subculture with which many members had become disenchanted.

The new constitution was an amalgam of ideas from other churches fused with the members' own beliefs of what a church ought to be. They stated their purpose this way:

> This church, as one unit in the larger Body of Christ, joins in the common purpose to be God's instrument in this world. As such, it is to provide both the opportunity and incentive for the worship of God, to proclaim the Good News of salvation in Jesus Christ, to foster maturity in believers, to provide loving fellowship for all, and to minister to the needs of the whole man.

(For more of the LaSalle constitution see Appendix A.)

Actually, the constitution was only the "charter" of LaSalle Street Church. On retreats and in cell groups, during Sunday night forums and informal discussions, members had brainstormed and debated how a congregation should express itself in activities intrinsic to the Church. Over the past turbulent decade, idea after idea had been weighed, winnowed, adapted, and readapted in both rhetoric and practice. In the process various position papers had been written— mostly by Bill and the other staff. They were never formally endorsed but used only as catalysts to provoke thought and action. After the church became independent, these papers were brought together under "A Short Philosophy of Our Major Activities" and distributed to the membership. They were divided into five areas: worship, education, fellowship, evangelism, and social concern. (For the complete text of these papers see Appendices B-F.)

Worship headed the list, for, they said, "We must be worshipers before we become workers."

Throughout the '60s worship at LaSalle had evolved from a simplistic, experience-centered, cliche-ridden, dull ritual to a rich and a varied liturgy mined from various cultural and denominational traditions.

The transformation was obvious to the eye. A set of Lutheran altar furniture made the front look more churchy. The altar, two pulpits for a divided chancel, twin candelabras, and a large cross were obtained for $400 from First St. Paul's Lutheran Church, which was refurnishing its new sanctuary.

The new cross covered up part of the lettering of John 3:16 that Moody Church had placed across the front. The rest of the lettering was painted over. "We still believe in the verse," Bill explained. "But many of us feel it has been misused to foster an easy believism."

The organ and choir were moved to the back balcony where they had been before the church had been purchased from the Swedish Lutherans. Omer Reese felt the music would be more meaningful with the choir out of view. Without robes, choir members did appear as a mixed lot of sizes, hair styles, and dress (from blue jeans to tailored suits).

The evolvement of the order of worship had come less smoothly.

In the old days planning the worship service had been a simple affair. The music director picked out two or three songs for the congregation and rehearsed the choir to sing a special number, usually a hymn with familiar beats and rhythm. The minister selected a responsive reading from the back of the hymnal and added his sermon topic. Sunday after dreary Sunday the same order was followed.

After the new breed took over, the pendulum swung the other way. People weren't kidding when they said, "You need a new road map every Sunday to keep up with the order of worship." Also, attempts at "relevance," such as the prayer litany which thanked God for "crispy, crunchy potato chips," seemed irreverent to the more serious-minded.

Now, a worship committee met regularly to plan the Sunday morning service. Anyone could come, but an artist, a creative writer, a musician, someone with good theological insights, general workers, a

131

pastoral intern, and the pastor were usually present. The pastor defined his message in a sentence or two. A response (the hoped-for result of the sermon) was formulated through group discussion. They brainstormed various possibilities for the call to worship, hymns, Scripture reading, prayers, liturgy, choir and solo, special features, and so on. Then each accepted an assignment in accordance with his gift to create or select an element in the service.

In exploring church history, LaSalle discovered that from its beginning Christianity had used visual art to depict great themes of the faith. Consequently, artistically talented members were urged to glorify God with their gifts by preparing banners, posters, and paintings that would enhance the worship services and brighten the fellowship hall. One Easter, for example, the sanctuary ceiling was aflutter with colorful banners that portrayed 18 resurrection symbols. A dictionary of meanings was included in the bulletin; for example, *Alpha and Omega*: Greek for Christ as the Beginning and End of all things; *Strawberry*: Symbol of righteousness; *Pomegranate tree*: Christian unity and the Resurrection.

Nor was worship limited to Sunday morning. Talented members wrote, scripted, and produced Biblical dramas as musicals and operas, utilizing both stage and film action. The popular Old Testament musical, "Esther," played to capacity audiences for double performances and drew standing ovations. Representatives from the Jewish Anti-Defamation League proclaimed it the best they had ever seen.

Like the proverbial old gray mare, education wasn't what it used to be at LaSalle either. Affirming that education that is Christian will involve the whole person, the working paper concluded that "a teaching of Scripture that is not internalized and applied is inadequate learning." Consequently, the church devised an educational program that involved doing (directed experiences, games, dramatic participation) or observing (demonstrations, field trips, exhibits) rather than symbolizing (film and recordings, visual symbols, lectures).

One example was the "Real Life Samaritan." The leader asked the mostly black group to pretend they were in Lincoln Park at night. The drama began with the mugging of a white boy by three blacks, who took his wallet and shoes. As he lay wounded, a well-dressed white and a minister in clerical collar "passed by on the other side." Then a poor Cabrini-Green black arrived, summoned an ambulance, accompanied the victim to the hospital, and paid the emergency room charges.

The Sunday school from nursery age through high school remained mostly black. Teachers were free to use whatever curriculum they wished or to improvise their own. David C. Cook was the most acceptable because, as Bill noted, "It contains pictures and activities with which blacks can identify." In keeping with the belief that "the greatest lessons in life are caught and not taught," many teachers spent more time with their children outside of class than inside. For instance, Walter Taylor, the president of a warehouse franchising company, took his boys to McDonald's for hamburgers after church and then to the zoo, a museum, or a ball game.

The Fellowship Hour continued to provide informal inspiration, information, and a sharing of views. Arthur Volle was chairperson (an example of the way terminology had changed) of a committee responsible for scheduling a variety of program leaders and panels from both within and without the membership. A random list of bookings:

"The Christian and Nationalism" by Richard Rung, a professor at Wheaton College.

"Women's Liberation" by a panel of LaSalle men and women.

"World Missions" by David Howard, Foreign Missions Director of Inter-Varsity.

"Tutoring at LaSalle" by Judi Hultman, director of the church's tutoring program.

Sunday evening forums usually offered a choice of two subjects: a Biblical book study and a contemporary topic relating to Christianity. A forum usually ran from three to six weeks. A sample of titles: "The Implications of the Charismatic Movement for the Church"; "The Christian and Moral Dilemmas"; "Building Family Relationships"; "Modern Mythology in C. S. Lewis, Tolkien and others"; "Introductory Course in Biblical Prophecy"; and "Death and Dying."

In the summer when the days were long the adults held forums on

133

the grassy beachfront and also played volleyball or went swimming.

Regarding outreach, it was the view of LaSalle that traditional evangelism was too shallow, that too much of it was done out of duty and not in the interest of the total needs of persons. They saw, though, that many in the church had overreacted and were not sharing Christ verbally. Hence, the need for a fresh statement on evangelism and its importance: "The unique contribution which Christians, individually and collectively, can make in this world is to help people come to a personal relationship with God through Jesus Christ. If this be true, evangelism should always be high on the agenda of the church and the believer."

The key to evangelism, LaSalle thought, "is to get the 'body of Christ' to function as God intended." While acknowledging that God could work through the efforts of a small group or through a person who confronts strangers on the street, the church felt that friendship evangelism—sharing Christ with neighbors and co-workers—was most normal.

One of the many persons reached through friendship evangelism was Eileen, a Ph.D. candidate in German literature at the University of Chicago. Eileen came from a prominent family in Evanston. She had attended church as a girl and was having intellectual doubts about Christianity when a friend invited her into LaSalle's south-side cell group. Through this group she became aware of a dimension in human relationships that only Christ could offer. After a conference with Bill she made a personal commitment of faith and applied for membership in the church.

LaSalle had long been aware of the gap between "soul winners" and "Social Gospelers." Much trial and trauma and study of the Scriptures and church history had led to the conviction that by itself the proclamation of the Gospel is insufficient. Study and observation of various Protestant social-action groups had led them to pronounce the same verdict on the other extreme. During the racial crisis liberal Protestants had moved into the neighborhood with ambitious programs. By 1970 they were fizzling out.

Consequently, LaSalle sought to develop a balanced ministry that

134

would encompass both the spiritual and the social. They believed that Christian social concern must include social reconciliation, social relief (welfare), and social reform (sociopolitical action). This would involve ministry to individuals, institutions, and the state.

There was little preaching or teaching in the average Evangelical church on an individual Christian's responsibility beyond personal piety and honesty. And the full implications of personal honesty were not often spelled out (deceptive pricing of products by a Christian merchant, for example). LaSalle felt "the church must develop a social consciousness within the church community by constant education, admonition, and encouragement in every area and age level of church life."

The membership should be encouraged to participate in community organizations, service clubs, political groups, etc. Traditionally, Evangelicals had said, "If people need help, let them come to us." So a church could piously say it had never denied aid to anyone who was sincere, meaning it had given some charity to all who came personally seeking aid. LaSalle said, "The church should regularly evaluate the relief needs of her neighbors and seek to creatively care by expanding existing efforts and creating new programs." (Examples of evangelism and social concern at LaSalle are given in chapters that follow.)

While LaSalle was hammering out its position papers on ministry, Jim Johnson had continued telling the church's story. Among those showing interest was Arthur DeMoss, a Philadelphia insurance executive. DeMoss' Liberty Foundation had already given LaSalle $5,000 to use in planning a moderate-income housing development. Now he wanted to evaluate the effect Christian social concern had on evangelism. After discussing the idea further, DeMoss pledged that Liberty would finance a computerized survey of members and regular attenders at Elm-LaSalle. The survey would be under the direction of Dr. David Moberg, Chairperson of the Department of Sociology at Marquette University.

The survey sought to determine who LaSallers were, what they believed, how they felt about various issues related to Christianity and society, and directions they thought the church should take. The measuring tool was an 18-page questionnaire. It would be one of the most comprehensive studies ever made of a church congregation in the United States.

Among the 252 persons who completed questionnaires, 79 were LaSalle members or applicants for membership, 91 were regular attenders, and the balance were irregular attenders or visitors. The computer printout showed them to be:

Young (61 percent under 25; about 80 percent under 35); females outranking males (55 to 45 percent); two-thirds single and one-third married; and well-educated (51 percent college graduates; about 25 percent with some graduate school).

Predominantly Caucasian (237).

Generous (124 said they gave 10 percent or more to the church or religious causes).

Theologically conservative (193 classified themselves as fundamentalist or Evangelical; only 25 termed themselves liberal).

Changed by the church (144 said, "I have become more tolerant of people who differ from me"; 120 said, "I have recognized the need to be active in community life and politics"; 112 said, "I have realized my need for dependence upon other Christians"; 81 said, "I have learned how to worship"; 66 said, "I have a better understanding of the Bible and Christian doctrine"; 60 said, "I have become involved in helping meet men's social needs"; but only 40—a matter of concern to the staff—said, "I have become a more effective witness for Jesus Christ").

Attracted to LaSalle church in a variety of ways (checked in order of most influence with numerical ranking as follows: first, "recommended by a friend"; second, "reputation for social concern"; third, "conveniently located"; fourth, "desired involvement in an inner-city church"; fifth, "wanted a small church"; sixth, "had a reputation for the Gospel"; seventh, "knew one of the ministers"; eighth, "saw the church or its publicity and became curious about it"; ninth, "helped in one of its social services").

Influenced to become socially concerned (by lectures in the Fellow-

136

ship Hour—167; sermons—165; total impact of the church—128; studying the Bible—81; working in one of the church's ministries to the community—58; reading a Christian book heard about at church—52; attending a cell group—37; reading a secular book learned about at church—21).

Some other interesting revelations:

The church felt it was most important to minister to blacks, then college and university students, alienated youth subculture, elderly, international students, and Gold Coast residents.

Most "strongly agreed" or "agreed" that the church should continue to express social concern for individuals "even if they reject the call to salvation." (In his evaluation, Moberg noted that LaSalle rejected the concept "if they don't take the bait, then go and fish somewhere else.")

The majority disagreed that the main goal of every church service should be to evangelize non-Christians.

LaSallers tended to be conservative theologically but liberal politically. Around 80 percent said they believed "the Bible is the infallible Word of God because every word is inspired." Political attitudes according to numerical ranking were, first, independent liberal; second, moderate Republican; third, independent conservative; fourth, liberal Republican; fifth, conservative Republican; sixth, Democrat. A substantial number said attendance at LaSalle had led them to become more politically liberal.

Only two felt that the church should belong to a denomination, and even they were not strongly in favor of affiliation.

Only 18 said they had been at LaSalle over five years.

New Horizons

10

New Horizons

LASALLE STREET CHURCH IN THE EARLY '70S was like a patient who had survived a series of operations and had emerged from the hospital brimming with ambition, but limited in resources.

Bill was still plodding along in graduate school. Even with his family now living in the city, his time continued to be squeezed between church and studies.

He had had two more setbacks in his Ph.D. program. He had completed language requirements and taken five weeks of comprehensive exams in 1969. Then a year and a half into his dissertation he discovered a French monograph covering the same topic. A Ph.D. dissertation has to come from unplowed ground, so all his research and writing were wasted, and he had to start over on a new subject. He had hardly begun again when his major faculty adviser went on a sabbatical leave to Greece. He would have to wait until the professor returned.

Everyone at the church had been patient with him. They wanted their pastor to get a doctorate.

The membership was still highly transient. Several of the young doctors finished their training in Chicago and moved on to distant places. But the Wheaton short-termers and other establishment adults arriving in the late '60s all remained.

Consequently, the church was in better financial condition than ever. Offerings of five and six hundred dollars a week were not unusual. But this was not nearly enough to buy the building for the $95,000 price the Moody Church board had set. It was not even ample to pay staff salaries. The Leslies were making it only because Adrienne had returned to teaching.

Tutoring—now on Monday night—was going full steam. Wheaton College provided a bus for students who wanted to tutor. A few student tutors were coming from MBI. Bill had given the Institute's Practical Work Department a standing offer to supervise internships for students desiring training in urban ministries.

Fortunately for LaSalle and other inner-city churches, some Evangelical schools had already taken steps in this direction. Gilbert James, a pastor turned sociology professor at Asbury Seminary, set up the Urban Ministries Program for Seminarians (UMPS) under a get-started grant from the Lilly Foundation. Several seminaries—Anderson, Asbury, Bethel, Conservative Baptist, North Park, and the Associated Mennonite Biblical Seminaries—agreed to participate. Seminarians accepted for internships would receive course credit for a summer's work and a stipend of $800. The city churches and agencies under which they worked would provide staff direction and room and board.

James recognized that most Evangelical seminarians were from rural, small-town, and suburban backgrounds. They would have to be prepared for ministry in the big cities.

After a successful pilot program in New York, the first UMPS "class" for Chicago arrived in June, 1969. Already they had read books on urban society, politics, and minority subcultures. Now for five days they listened to social workers, urbanologists, and pastors such as Bill Leslie and David Mains. At the end of the week they took "The Plunge"—surviving on the streets for 48 hours with only pocket money.

LaSalle took two or three interns each year from the pool of UMPS seminarians. They organized basketball teams in the neighborhood, coached swimming classes, led Bible studies, took children on field trips around the city, served as counselors in day camps, visited lonely senior citizens, helped destitute persons cut through welfare tape, participated in worship services, and did countless other services.

The UMPS interns were a new class of seminarians. They tended to be more adventurous and innovative than their seminary peers. They were disposed to question traditional methods of ministry. They wanted to know if the church could "hack it" in the metropolis.

Take Jan Erickson, a flaxen-haired, blue-eyed Swedish girl from a Minneapolis suburb, who was assigned to LaSalle. During high school she had stopped attending church "because I questioned a lot of things." Then after three years at the University of Minnesota, she traveled around Europe for four months. In London she read C. S. Lewis' *Mere Christianity* and came to a solid conviction that Christianity was really true and worth a lifetime commitment. She returned home and after finishing college and a year at Bethel Seminary became an UMPS intern.

Jan's experiences in Europe made her more worldly wise than the typical UMPS participant. She was not as apprehensive as others when she left the Loop YMCA to begin The Plunge. She used 45¢ of her $4.00 allotment to buy a train ride to a Swedish area on the far-north side. She moved around the neighborhood savoring the familiar smells, talking to people as if she lived there. Then she walked four miles south to touristy Old Town and looked for a cheap hotel. Finding nothing she could afford, she walked on to the "Y" and used most of her remaining $3.55 for a room.

The next morning Jan walked back to Old Town and ran into a friendly bunch of sandaled youth her own age who said they were passing through Chicago. The drifters paid for her lunch and made no attempt to take advantage of her. They invited her to remain with them. "No, I'm moving on," she said and left the group to mingle with tourists and conventioneers. Occasionally, a man would stop her, make "suggestions," and offer money. Around 11:00 p.m. she was passing Jeff's Laugh-In Restaurant and Lounge on Wells Street and saw a sign in a window saying, "Waitress Wanted." Hungry and tired, she went in and asked for Jeff. "I've waited tables before," she

143

said. "Can I work for just tonight and earn a little money for bread?" "OK," he replied. "Seven dollars and tips."

Working from midnight to 8:00 a.m., she got $17 in tips, plus free supper and breakfast, and more propositions. When she finished work, Jeff said, "Look, you're too nice a girl to be roaming around this way." He and his girl friend took her to their apartment and gave her a bundle of clothes.

When she reported to UMPS headquarters and told her experiences, a fellow intern suggested she had been naive and foolish to go to the manager's apartment. "They only wanted to help me," she countered. "Not everybody is out to exploit you in the city."

Jan spent the remainder of the summer at LaSalle. She worked with senior citizens, paying them cheering visits, sharing her faith, taking them to the doctor and dentist, helping them buy nutritious food, and doing whatever else seemed necessary for lonely elders. In addition she worked in the youth day camp and served as a general "girl Friday" in other church programs.

The UMPS program was a real boost to LaSalle. But because it ran only during the summer, the church felt the necessity for year-round workers. Ron Cook had resigned to accept another position, and there was not enough money to hire a full-time replacement.

Letters were sent out inviting donor participation. The new Tyndale Foundation, headed by Kenneth Taylor, provided a grant, and college graduates were invited to apply.

One of the year-rounders who came in the '70s was Dan Good, a rural Pennsylvania youth of Mennonite and Baptist heritage who looked to some like a grown-up Oliver Twist. But he was not as innocent and unknowing as he appeared.

Dan had come to Wheaton College a typical fundamentalist youth who had been warned by his pastor to watch out for radical wolves. At Wheaton his world view was widened by exposure to students and professors from all parts of the Evangelical spectrum. His attitude toward social involvement was changed by a controversy over Senator Mark Hatfield and the lectures of a fiery Chinese professor.

Hatfield had been invited by a student committee to speak in chapel.

At the last minute the administration forced a switch in plans, saying the large chapel auditorium would not be available and the Oregon senator would have to speak from the smaller, older chapel. Student anger flamed when a story swept the campus that the administration had bowed to pressure from conservatives, upset because Hatfield opposed President Nixon's Vietnam policies. Amid student protests the administration stood firm.

Dan was still seething over the Hatfield incident when he took a sociology course under Ka Tong Gaw, a young Filipino of Chinese descent who had previously served as David Mains' associate at Circle Church. Gaw talked about his experiences in the inner city. He accused Evangelicals of racial discrimination and indifference toward the urban poor. He said Evangelicals had passed over the city in their zeal to evangelize people abroad. Dan Good listened and was stirred. When Larry Beal, a fellow student who was teaching Sunday school at LaSalle, mentioned a possible internship in social work, Dan, then a senior, applied immediately.

The city was totally unlike anything Dan had ever known. Crowds of people, none of whom would smile or speak. Vacant-eyed old men and women stumbling along the sidewalks. Bums sucking cheap wine in litter-strewn alleys. Homosexuals propositioning passersby. But most heart-touching were the swarms of black children around Cabrini-Green.

He was put in charge of the summer day-care camp. Mornings were spent at the church with arts, crafts, cooking, carpentry, and Bible studies. Afternoons, Dan and the UMPS workers took the kids to museums, parks, the beach, and other attractions.

Their favorite place was Adventureland, an amusement park in suburban Bloomingdale, an hour's drive from the church. Unfortunately, on one occasion Dan forgot to bring extra money. He arrived with 26 bouncy Cabrini-Green youngsters, psyched up for daredevil rides. He and the staff counted their money. They had only enough for 20 admissions. Dan explained the shortage and asked the kids to chip in. Now they had enough for 26, with 20¢ left over. Dan and one of the UMPS fellows agreed to remain outside.

When the others finally came out, Dan counted noses. Ten-year-old Jack was missing. Dan sent two boys to find him. When Jack returned, they got the boys in the vans and drove them back to the church through the heavy rush hour. When they stopped, someone yelled, "We left Bryan!" Bryan, 11, was one of the two sent to find Jack.

Dan unloaded the van and headed back into traffic. He found a scared little black boy waiting at the park gate. Putting an arm around his shaking shoulders, Dan assured, "We wouldn't leave you out here by yourself. Come on, I'll take you home." Dan took the boy to Cabrini-Green and made sure he was safe.

The climax of day camp was a visit to an Ohio farm, a new experience for the young blacks. They had never camped in a meadow and cooked over an open fire.

Discipline was easy. Dan had only to say, "If you do that again, you'll have to sleep outside by yourself." Accustomed to the bright lights of the city, the kids were petrified by the rural night.

Dan and 11-year-old Bryan became especially close. After returning to Chicago, Bryan spent the night at Dan's apartment. They cooked, went shopping together, then played games before going to bed. The next morning they were walking toward Cabrini-Green when Bryan remarked, "It's like a dream come true."

"What do you mean?" Dan asked, thinking he was referring to a dream he had had the night before.

"Martin Luther King dreamed that black and white would walk together. Now it's true, Dan. You're white, I'm black, and we're walking together, ain't we?"

Dan swallowed hard and his eyes misted up. "Yes, Bryan," he murmured. "For you and me it's true."

The year-round interns were of tremendous help. But none could fill a gaping hole in the staff which had been obvious for years, the need for a seasoned black staff member. Marj Branch had given vital assistance, but she had a demanding job in the Chicago school system. And she was a woman. More than anything, Cabrini-Green youth, 83 percent of whom lived in fatherless families, needed good male models.

146

Bill went to George Scheffer, Young Life's urban director in Chicago, and proposed a partnership. If Young Life would find a black man to direct youth programs at LaSalle, the church would raise half of his salary and expenses. Scheffer, who had recently suffered a beating by thugs, was going to Colorado to set up a Bible training school for black inner-city workers. He recommended to his successor, Bud Ipema, that the LaSalle offer be accepted. Young Life had never worked with just one church before, but Ipema and the Chicago Young Life board felt LaSalle was a deserved exception. If only a few black youth could be discipled and put into college for training to be Christian workers, it would be worth it.

Young Life sent its national urban director from Colorado Springs to serve on the LaSalle staff. Joe White was a husky black air force veteran who understood young blacks. Again, the Tyndale Foundation provided a financial grant, with other aid coming from South Park Church.

Joe spent a few weeks getting acquainted, then came to Bill with a conclusion.

"Man, some of these dudes don't have any vision bigger than becoming a pimp. Some of the older guys are pretty good basketball players, but the way they're going, they'll never make it to college."

"What do you have in mind?" Bill asked.

"Well, I was down in Bermuda last year leading the music for Tom Skinner. You wouldn't believe it, but the black kids there are way behind our kids here in sports. And they are strangers to basketball. I'd like to take eight of our older guys down and hold some basketball clinics. Some of the black Young Life staff members from the East will go along and take some of their guys. It'll be terrific fellowship for our guys."

Catching his breath, Bill gasped, "How much will it cost us?"

"If we take one of the church vans to the East Coast and catch the plane, we can hold it to $1,700."

Bill whistled, wondering why they couldn't go somewhere closer like Pittsburgh, and also thinking he had never been to Bermuda himself.

"Think of what it will do for our guys," Joe continued with mounting enthusiasm. "Most of them have never been out of the city. It'll be an adventure of a lifetime."

Now that he had overcome the shock, Bill was thinking of what financial supporters might say about the expenditure. Finally, he said, "I'll talk to our board. If they say OK, then I guess you can go." The board agreed—reluctantly and skeptically.

The team was overwhelmed. "Ya mean it? Ya really mean it?" Harry Jones kept asking. Harry was a junior at Cooley High, making better grades than most, and living with his mother and seven brothers and sisters near Cabrini-Green.

Harry's sidekick, Speed, was jumping for joy and pounding everybody on the back. "Let's go! Let's go! Look out, Bermuda. Here we come."

Still wondering about the wisdom of the jaunt, Bill joined Chuck Hogren at the church to give them a send-off on a cold morning in February.

When they returned ten days later and gave a report to their families and friends in the church fellowship hall, all of Bill's doubts vanished.

"It was great, just great," Harry said with tears in his eyes. "We held six clinics for about 800 kids. They loved it. Did everything we told them. But what I really liked was the chance to help somebody else. We all know how Reverend Leslie and Chuck and LaSalle Church has helped us. And we appreciate it. But there ain't no joy like helping kids the way we did in Bermuda."

Bermuda was just the beginning. Joe picked up Bob Davenport's "Wandering Wheels" idea. After a short pilot run, he took 23 young blacks on a bike trip to Muskegon, Michigan, stopping overnight with Christian families and also camping in the woods along the way. (The bikes were purchased with donor gifts.) A few months later they rafted the white waters of Wisconsin's Green River. Then as a grand finale they went to the Young Life summer camp in Colorado where they climbed a snow-capped mountain.

Joe also made regular swings around Evangelical colleges in the area, rapping with around 20 young blacks about their future plans. Most were from middle- and upper-class families, and the city was as strange to them as it was to suburban whites. Joe brought them into the city to help with the youth programs at LaSalle and took them on trips with neighborhood boys. The fellowship and intermixing raised the ambitions of inner-city blacks as nothing ever had. They began to see possibilities of attending college themselves and training for youth ministries. Harry Jones was the first of a half-dozen to actually go, enrolling on a scholarship at North Park College.

The Tyndale Foundation had given only a get-started grant for the cooperative venture with Young Life. They hoped that other donors would catch the vision and pick up the work in future years. Going into the third year, 1973, the project was deep in the red. Seven of the ten-speed bikes purchased for the "Wandering Wheels" trips had been stolen, and no money was available to replace them. Worse, Joe's salary was in arrears for $3,600.

When Joe resigned to work as a counselor at North Park College, there were no funds to hire a successor. The two-year experiment had cost $30,000, but no one could say it hadn't paid off in redirecting the lives of many young blacks.

Housing Hassles

11

Housing Hassles

CHANGE HAD CONTINUED at a dizzying pace on the near-north side while LaSalle was involved with neighborhood youth. Old houses seemed to be replaced overnight by big signs announcing new high rises. The church was practically a congregation of commuters. There was not one homeowner among the few members living in the neighborhood.

The Leslies had continued to lease the town house on Crilly Court while renting out their own home in Wheaton. They found it was not easy being absentee landlords.

After their first tenants had moved out, the house stayed vacant three months. This threw their budget into a tailspin. Then it happened that their new tenants were black, the first of their race to move into the Wheaton neighborhood. Dr. Ozzie Edwards, an old friend of Bill's, also happened to be the first black on the Wheaton College faculty.

Bill and Adrienne saw the Edwardses as a godsend, but some of their former neighbors didn't. "Maybe we'll picket your house," one neighbor told Adrienne. "Just kidding, of course," he added. Another couple were more upset. They feared a big drop in property values. That didn't happen. As it turned out, the Edwardses became one of the most popular families in the neighborhood.

The next renters, white, left the patio torn up, the walls scarred, and the parquet wood floors dented from rocks the children had thrown around the house. The Leslies were dismayed. They had hoped to sell the house and buy in the city. Now it would take two or three thousand dollars to put it in marketable shape—money they didn't have. The Wheaton cell group—principally the Turners, Volles, and Boardmans—did the repairs without charge, and the house was sold.

The help couldn't have come at a more opportune time, for the Leslies were facing a crisis. The house they were leasing and most others on Crilly Court had been purchased by a land trust. Rent was to double when their lease ran out on September 5, 1971—the date they were expecting their fourth child.

Land values were still skyrocketing on the Near North side. The Leslies felt they should buy as a testimony of their commitment to stay. But where? And how? The amount realized on their Wheaton house wasn't enough for the large down payment which would be required for an older home.

While they were praying for direction, a realtor neighbor called to say he had a listing right on Crilly Court. It was one of three houses not bought by the trust. The elderly owners had died within a month of each other, and he was the executor of the estate. "Only a nephew is left, and he doesn't want it. You can get it very reasonable, but it will need a little fixing up."

It did indeed. The old couple had subdivided the house into tiny cubicles for roomers—a gross violation of the single-family residential zoning. Radiators leaked. The plumbing was rusty and antiquated. The wiring was dangerous. Shades were torn and some windows and transoms broken, with newspapers taped over holes. The steps leading upstairs trembled when used. Almost every door hung on one hinge. The original coal furnace in the basement was a fire hazard. The black floors and the cruddy pea-green and garish-pink walls repelled the eye.

With all this, the down payment was still more than the Leslies could swing.

Still, they prayed, "Lord, if it's Your will, You'll have to provide the money."

Within the week an old Wheaton College friend called. "The Lord has blessed me in business," he said. "If you ever need a loan, I'd love to let you have it interest free."

They bought the house, reserving a modest amount for repairs.

Now they needed a contractor. The first to look pronounced the house a "real white elephant" and told Adrienne, "Lady, you have good ideas. You just need three times the money."

Again, miracles happened. A teacher friend directed them to a semiretired contractor who took only jobs he enjoyed. John Clausen looked at the job and said, "Well, the Lord has been good to me. This will give me the chance to pay off some of my debts. I'll tear out the walls and redo the plumbing and electrical for whatever you can afford to pay me. Maybe friends can help with the redecorating."

LaSalle members helped gladly. They came in at night and shoveled out debris from the walls the contractor's crew had smashed. They put up shelves, repaired doors, installed new glass, scraped away old paint, and repainted all the walls and floors. In the process they uncovered a beautiful stained-glass skylight situated on the wall above the stairs.

As soon as the outside doors could be locked, the Leslies moved in. The remodeling continued through the summer. Finally, everything except Bill's basement office was finished—the day before Adrienne went to the hospital for the birth of their fourth child, Scott.

The pastor and his family now had a home of their own. The congregation still did not. The old church remained on the market. The people kept expecting any Sunday to see a "Sold" sign on the front.

Bill and Chuck Hogren took the problem to the city planner in the downtown Civic Center. "We're hoping you will recommend that the department of housing award us a church site on land purchased by urban renewal," Bill said.

The official smiled, "Some of the churches that ran out when it was bad now want back in. You have a good track record in staying and helping the community. I think we can help you, but you'll have to work with us. The people who make the decisions are very concerned about ecclesiastical sprawl that holds down the tax base. They want to maximize land use in urban renewal areas."

"We understand that," Bill said. "One idea I had when I was at Moody Church was to build a high rise over the sanctuary. We're thinking along the same lines at LaSalle. Maybe use the first two floors for church activities and a community center. Rent the upper floors to senior citizens or moderate-income families. Use the income to pay off the mortgage. Of course, we couldn't finance anything that big ourselves. We'd need backing and endorsement from the city and state housing authorities."

"Good, good. I'd suggest apartments for the elderly. We have a real need there. Since most old folks don't own cars, we could waive some of the parking requirements and reduce the site size required.

"Here's how it could be handled," the planner continued with rising enthusiasm. "You'd form a partnership with a group of investors looking for a tax shelter. They'd put up 10 percent and the federal government 90 percent. They'd get a tax write-off in yearly depreciation for the entire amount while the loan was being repaid."

The planner pulled out a map of the area and pinpointed three possible sites. Bill and Chuck left the office riding a crest of confidence.

Everyone at the church liked the plan, although some made comments about helping the rich get richer through tax shelters. "So we don't like the way the system operates," Bill countered. "OK. But if we can't change it, let's use it for the good of the people in the neighborhood."

They voted to go ahead. Bill went to one of the top architectural firms in Chicago, Loebl Schlossman, Bennett, and Dart, and appealed to their civic conscience. The prestigious firm agreed to do the preliminary plans at no charge.

Meanwhile, another housing idea was germinating at LaSalle Street Church. Marj Branch had repeatedly warned that the wide disparity in residential housing around the church was sure to precipitate more unrest and trouble. "You can't have the Gold Coast and Cabrini-Green facing one another," she said. "There has to be some modification in housing between."

The National Advisory Commission on Civil Disorders had cited

156

the housing problems of the inner city as a major factor in urban unrest and noted,

> The housing problem is particularly acute in the minority ghettos. Nearly two-thirds of all non-white families living in the central cities today live in neighborhoods marked with substandard housing and general urban blight. Two major factors are responsible.
>
> First: Many ghetto residents simply cannot pay the rent necessary to support decent housing. In Detroit, for example, over 40 percent of the non-white occupied units in 1960 required rent of over 35 percent of the tenants' income.
>
> Second: Discrimination prevents access to many non-slum areas, particularly the suburbs, where good housing exists. In addition, by creating a "back pressure" in the racial ghettos, it makes it possible for landlords to break up apartments for denser occupancy, and keeps prices and rents of deteriorated ghetto housing higher than they would be in a truly free market.

Federal programs, the Commission said, "have been able to do comparatively little to provide housing for the disadvantaged." The Commission recommended that "federal programs must be given a new thrust aimed at overcoming the prevailing patterns of racial segregation."

The near-north side seemed ready-made for a consortium of churches to act. But some group had to lead. Why not LaSalle? Yes, why not? the members decided. Decent housing that low-to-moderate income people could afford was certainly in the purview of ministering to the whole person.

Leaders of neighborhood churches were contacted and a list of possible sponsors drawn up.

Bill and Chuck took the list to the Civic Center and asked for guidance on how to proceed. "Clear it with the politicians," the official advised.

There were two major political factions on the near-north side: the Regular or Daley Democrats and the Independent Democrats. The leader of the Regular Democrats was adamantly opposed to the inclu-

157

sion of a certain church in the consortium. "The people there are against the city administration," he explained.

"That doesn't mean they shouldn't be a sponsor," Bill replied. "We can't let politics or theology or race divide us. This must be a community project." The Daley man was unconvinced. Fortunately he retired from business a few months later and moved out of the state.

Working under Bill's leadership, LaSalle convened an ad hoc committee of representatives from interested churches. Bill felt the entry fee for participation should be held to around $250. The blacks insisted on a $1,000 minimum. "This will keep out potential troublemakers," they said.

Five churches came up with the money and elected three representatives each to the board of the Chicago-Orleans Housing Corporation: LaSalle Street, St. Matthew's Methodist, St. Dominic's Catholic, Fourth Presbyterian, and Holy Family Lutheran. The board then met and unanimously elected Bill chairperson.

Their intentions were to build three or four multistory connecting buildings in an eye-pleasing court complex for integrated living. The apartments would be of varying sizes for singles, couples, and families of different incomes. They wanted to avoid the public housing concept of boxing together people on the bottom rung of the economic ladder. They desired facilities that would aid in developing community loyalty and individual pride.

Now besides graduate school and leadership of LaSalle, Bill had the administrative responsibility of two multimillion-dollar housing projects (approximately $3 million for the LaSalle Church senior-citizens high rise and $8 million for the consortium's development). Adding to his pyramiding load came fresh criticism from the Evangelical camp. Some who had finally come around to admitting the rightness of social ministries said that the housing consortium involved LaSalle in an "unholy alliance" with churches of questionable orthodoxy. The criticism had come up before. Bill's reply was that "where theology was not involved, LaSalle would work for the betterment of mankind with any person or group with integrity. Where beliefs were involved, the church would be more selective."

Beyond this, Bill had no time to argue the question of separatism versus alliance. The complexities of the housing programs were just becoming apparent.

The city planner had made it sound easy. It wasn't. Almost every week there were office visits to make, bureaucratic snafus to unravel, forms to complete. Each procedural step had to be approved by city, state, and federal officials. Not only were their offices scattered around town, but some were not on speaking terms with their counterparts in other levels of government. Besides the red tape, there were board meetings with representatives from the other churches and conferences with community groups. The meetings seemed endless. The danger of misunderstanding was great when so many different persuasions and interests were involved. And the possibility of compromise with personal convictions was ever present as Bill walked the narrow ledge of diplomacy.

Along the way he learned some principles: (1) Speak to both Christians and non-Christians on the basis of self-interest. He would tell church groups (including suburban churches who asked his views on open housing), "Unless you do something, your children will be taxed so heavily for law enforcement, they will repudiate the heritage you've given them." The city and state officials wanted to keep the federal money pipeline open. He could tell them, "The successful completion of our programs will pave the way for more participation." (2) Dress conservatively. One official frankly advised him to shave off the new beard he had grown during summer vacation in 1971. (3) Don't give up. Keep making adjustments to satisfy official specifications.

By 1973 the way appeared clear. Urban renewal had allocated a site for the consortium's Chicago-Orleans Housing Corporation's complex. The seven-acre plot was located on the far side of Wells, directly west of the church. Another three-acre plot on the eastern side of Wells and to the south was tentatively reserved for the high rise.

Then just when they were talking of a groundbreaking date for the consortium's project, the Nixon administration slapped a "temporary" freeze on federal housing funds.

159

LaSalle had continued to use the old building, paying Moody Church $255 a month to cover prorated insurance, maintenance, and custodial supplies and care.

Moody Church had had a pastoral change. George Sweeting had moved down LaSalle Street to become the new president of Moody Bible Institute. Sweeting had put Moody Church on the upturn and broadened its outreach. Much more than a citadel for fundamentalist preaching, the church was now ministering more directly to neighborhood residents. Enrollment in the day-care center was growing. School teachers tutored slow learners before prayer meeting on Wednesday night. Other members led Bible studies in surrounding high rises. Blacks were being welcomed enthusiastically into the membership.

The new senior pastor was Warren Wiersbe. He was younger than Sweeting and older than Bill Leslie and David Mains, who knew him from Youth for Christ days. He had once edited YFC's monthly magazine and had done "Gospel magic" with Mains. While he couldn't endorse all their concepts of church ministry, Wiersbe felt a close bond with them as brothers and colaborers in Christian service. He wanted especially to resolve the LaSalle building impasse to the satisfaction of all concerned. The new pastor asked the Moody Church clerk for a record of past actions relating to the building. Then he requested that it be taken off the market while attempts were made to negotiate a sale to LaSalle.

In June, 1973, Moody Church dropped the price from $95,000 to $75,000. The Tyndale Foundation pledged a $25,000 gift if the two churches would each be responsible for an equal amount. Under Wiersbe's leadership, Moody Church raised its share with the understanding that all monies from the sale would be used for refurbishing the larger church's facilities. When LaSalle had difficulty, Tyndale offered an additional $10,000 if the smaller congregation could come up with $15,000 by July 31.

The money came in. Everyone was happy. LaSalle now owned the old building. Moody Church was freed of a long-standing headache and had $75,000 for much-needed renovation.

LaSalle celebrated with a special thanksgiving service during which the deed was formally passed by a representative of Moody Church to the chairperson of LaSalle's board. This was followed by a performance of Gabrielli's "Jubilato Deo" by LaSalle's brass and choral choirs and the Chamber Singers from Ridgewood High School where Omer Reese taught music.

Everybody was praising the Lord.

Doing Justice

12

Doing Justice

THE CELEBRATION OVER, the LaSalle members turned their attention back to the struggles of their neighbors. One of the deep-seated problems they attacked was the need for law and justice. Blacks, Puerto Ricans, and poor whites complained of police brutality and an uncaring court system. Police steamed about lack of citizen cooperation. Law-and-order types flailed liberals for blaming society instead of criminals for the ever-increasing crime rate. All while everyone seemed to live in constant fear of muggers, rapists, and snipers, especially around Cabrini-Green, where two police officers had been shot and killed from an upper-story window.

The National Advisory Commission on Civil Disorders had cited "deep hostility between police and ghetto communities" as "a primary cause" of the riots of the '60s, while explaining:

> It is wrong to define the problem solely as hostility to police. In many ways the policeman only symbolizes much deeper problems.
>
> The policeman in the ghetto is a symbol not only of law, but of the entire system of law enforcement and criminal justice.
>
> As such, he becomes the tangible target for grievances against shortcomings throughout that system; against assembly-line justice in teeming lower courts; against wide disparities in sentences;

against antiquated corrections facilities; against the basic inequities imposed by the system on the poor—to whom, for example, the option of bail means only jail.*

To all this, Chuck Hogren could say a fervent "Amen."

Talking with boys he taught in Sunday school and tutored on Monday evening, visiting their families in dingy apartments, observing the behavior of police, and occasionally going to court for an accused offender had made him aware of injustices he had not known before.

A welfare mother threatened with physical harm by a loan shark. A 15-year-old boy, whose family could not make bail, brutalized by homosexuals and hardened criminals in jail. The young brother of Harold Brown shot in a street fight by two police officers and left to die on the sidewalk.

This was not the WASP world from which Chuck came. His family and friends knew their rights and were not likely to suffer injustice. They had good credit ratings and could buy from reputable stores. If arrested for a law violation, their signature was usually enough for release until trial date. If not, they could almost always make bail. If legal aid was desired, most had an understanding and affordable family lawyer.

The cry for law and order and crackdown on crime was mainly coming from this world—a world which, Chuck concluded, did not fully understand the problems of impoverished minorities.

Until coming to LaSalle Chuck thought free legal aid was readily available to the poor and indigent. In theory this was true. There was a staff of public defenders. But they were usually just out of law school and working to gain experience. When a lucrative offer to join a good law firm came, most usually moved on, leaving their places to be filled by the inexperienced.

Experienced or not, a public defender could not give a client comprehensive help and keep up with his case load. Too often a defender would simply advise his client to plead guilty in hope of getting probation, even when he had a good chance of proving the person innocent. A deal was worked out with the prosecutor in which the accused was allowed to plead guilty to a lesser charge.

Plea bargaining supposedly saved time by keeping court dockets from becoming unbearably clogged. But it left an uninformed client completely at the mercy of the lawyers. If charged with a misdemeanor, he would have only a couple of minutes with the defender, then appear briefly before a judge for sentence. A defender might schedule one or two interviews for a felony case, but unless defense witnesses were readily available, he usually suggested the speedier route.

Chuck felt that for some clients plea bargaining was the best solution. But for others, copping a plea simply added to the problem. Typically, a poor black accused of a felony and unable to make bail would have lost his job by the time his case came to trial. Released and back on the street with a conviction on his record, his job prospects were practically zero. Welfare would keep him alive, but if he felt he had received a raw deal, he would be tempted to turn to street crime—even if he had been innocent the first time. This meant his chances of going back to court were good. So the court jam got bigger. The crime rate kept rising. The police became busier. The solid citizens got angrier. And the victims got more frustrated and desperate. There was simply not enough justice to go around.

Chuck wasn't at LaSalle long before word got around that he was a sympathetic lawyer, one who wanted to help people. Requests for aid snowballed. "Can you get my boy out of jail? His cell mate is threatening to kill him." "Please don't let the finance company take our stove and refrigerator." "Tell the police my kid didn't know the car was hot. He just went along for a joyride. They'll listen to you." And on and on.

Chuck's training and practice were in probate and real estate law, a well-paying specialty the poor hardly needed. Inexorably, inevitably, his interests moved to legal problems more common to the LaSalle community. He was affected by more than the needs of desperate people reaching out for help, though. He was also changed by the sermons and discussions at the church about Scripture and justice.

Chuck checked "justice" in a concordance and was astonished at how frequently the term appears in the Bible. He meditated on the sermons of the Old Testament prophets. He was challenged by Micah's call to "do justice."

He reread the Gospels and was struck by what Jesus said on the subject. He noted that while commending the Pharisees for scrupulously tithing every product of their labors, even garden herbs, Jesus had charged, "You neglect to obey the really important teachings of the Law, such as justice and mercy and honesty." Certainly God was for justice.

The idea for a legal aid clinic surfaced at LaSalle. No other Evangelical church was known to have one. When Evangelicals talked about justice, they almost always spoke of it in connection with salvation. Jesus had met God's demands for justice by paying the penalty for human guilt and sin in His atoning death on the Cross.

LaSalle went beyond this emphasis. Everyone there was also for legal aid to the materially poor. The only questions were who and how.

Chuck volunteered to be the director, the lawyer, and the workhorse. Tyndale extended $10,000 for the first year's operation, which included $5,200 for Chuck's salary—a fraction of the going rate in private practice. Secretarial and office expense would run costs beyond the $10,000 and have to be made up by other donations.

The LaSalle people felt the clinic should be controlled by the church but function under a separate board. A minority of board members would come from outside the church.

Bar association rules required that clients be restricted to persons with incomes below the federal government's poverty level. Because most neighborhood people in this classification lived in the public housing project, they incorporated as the Cabrini-Green Legal Aid Clinic.

Chuck was already fully licensed to practice in city, county, and state courts and had taken several courses in criminal law. But because he had been specializing in probate, he signed up for an intensive post-graduate course in criminal law at the Northwestern Law School.

Now to rent an office, since church facilities were inadequate. Bill spread the word among other neighborhood churches and agencies. Fr. Mark Santo at St. Dominic's called to say they had space in their convent. A nominal $100 monthly rent was agreed on. Gina Berg, a young, black LaSalle member, who had helped in the Yellow House, was hired as Chuck's secretary and research assistant.

Soon after the clinic opened in February, 1973, a group of black law students from DePaul came to talk with Chuck about a partnership. "We've organized ourselves as Preventive Legal Services," they said. "We're trying to 'prevent' legal problems by providing information and advice for neighborhood people. But we can't try cases in court because none of us is a lawyer yet. Therefore, we'd like to work with you. We'll gather evidence, interview witnesses, and help prepare cases for you to try."

Chuck accepted their offer gladly. Others from LaSalle gave time. For example, Dick Harbaugh, a corporation attorney, helped Chuck with cases relating to his expertise. Don Denton did some library research and ran down hard-to-find witnesses.

The report of the first year's operation showed the clinic had handled 233 cases—all persons with annual incomes of $4,000 or less who could not afford to hire standard legal help. The clinic had brought 132 of these cases to a satisfactory conclusion. Of 89 criminal prosecutions, 54 had been dismissed or given a verdict of not guilty.

The DePaul students in Preventive Legal Services carried a full school load. Because their time was limited, Chuck had to do some of the legwork. It was not unusual for him to devote to a case dozens of hours, scattered across several months, before marking the file "closed." Often his painstaking work spelled the difference between prison and freedom for clients.

Take the case of the prosecutors with the bad memories.

It began when three teenage boys were arrested and charged with robbing a delivery person. The victim claimed they had come up behind him with guns, knocked him down some steps, and taken his receipt book thinking it was his wallet. Chuck knew all three from activities at the church. One was Harold Brown.

169

At the preliminary hearing the accuser could only identify one of the three as an assailant. But the arresting officer said he had talked to an eyewitness who had seen all three at the scene of the crime. The judge ordered them held over for trial.

The boys were in jail two months before their parents could raise $500 bail money for each. A few days later one told Chuck he had heard through the neighborhood grapevine that a boy named Jack Oakum had admitted the crime. Chuck found young Oakum and asked if it was true.

"Sure, man," he said. "But it didn't happen the way the pigs said. I was standing at that dark corner when I felt a hand on my shoulder. Almost scared me out of my skin. I whirled around and knocked him down the stairwell. Then I hit him again 'cause I was afraid he might get back at me."

"Did you take his receipt book?" Chuck asked.

"No, I didn't take nuthin'. I just took off runnin'."

"You don't want three innocent guys to go to jail, do you?" Chuck asked.

Oakum shook his head.

"OK, then come with me and tell what happened. If they bring a charge, I'll help you."

Because the youth trusted Chuck, he agreed to go.

Two prosecutors for the state listened to his story. "We'll arrange a lie detector test," they promised Chuck. "If he passes, your clients are in the clear."

About a month later Chuck was notified that the case had been assigned to a new prosecutor and judge. He told them about the confession, and the prosecutor promised to look in the files. Then he reported back to Chuck that the notes from the previous interview with Oakum were missing. Trying not to show the disgust he felt, Chuck said, "I'll get him to come in and see you."

The youth was now uncooperative. "No, man, I ain't goin' back there. I was lucky they didn't lock me up the first time."

Chuck went to the judge and got a subpoena. He found Oakum again and served the legal papers. "I ain't going," was the determined response. "Then I'll have to get an arrest warrant and have the police pick you up," Chuck said.

The police claimed they couldn't find him. "He's at the address I told you," Chuck said. "But I'll go check on him again."

Chuck returned and reported, "He's there now." The police left and came back a short time later with the same story.

Trying a different tack, Chuck had the two prosecutors who had first interviewed Oakum subpoenaed. They came to court on separate days and gave the same testimony: the defense lawyer (Chuck) had brought a black youth to the office, but they couldn't remember his name or the gist of the conversation.

Chuck felt they were lying to keep from admitting that the records of the confession had been carelessly lost. The case dragged on for almost a year. One of the three defendants was stabbed in a street fight and spent two months in the hospital. After he was pronounced able to stand trial, they went to court. Even without young Oakum's confession admitted in evidence, the judge found all three not guilty. They were free, but during the delay all three had lost their jobs.

Not every case involved such an obvious miscarriage of justice. Chuck had a pretty good perception of a client's guilt, although a couple of times he was wrong. Regardless, he felt every one who came to the clinic deserved the best legal representation possible.

The clinic came on hard times in 1974, when a second Tyndale grant for $5,000 was exhausted. With only $100 of pledged monthly support, Chuck, it seemed, would have to seek other employment. The church covenanted to fast and pray for a week. Unexpectedly, both *Christianity Today* and he *Chicago Tribune* did stories on the clinic. An editor at *Christianity Today* saw the story before it was put into type and sent a check for $112. Additional help came from readers of both publications—enough to keep the clinic going three more months.

In 1975 the clinic was still operating from month to month with 22 DePaul law students assisting through Preventive Legal Services. Only one of the 22 was white, and he was one of only two professing Christians in the group.

171

Several of the black law students were church dropouts. One young woman frankly told Chuck, "While I admire you and the people at LaSalle Church, I see churches as irrelevant and uncaring.

"My uncle is pastor of a black Baptist church. Ninety-five percent of his people are on welfare. The last time I was there I heard him tell them, 'I know your life is hard. I know you have rats and roaches and live in firetraps. I know you are being ripped off by the Man every day. But don't worry. All your troubles and sorrows will soon be over and you'll have your mansion in the sky.' There he stood in a tailor-made suit, owning a new car, living in a beautiful home, and saying that. I argued with him for two hours afterward, telling him he should be ashamed of himself for not raising the ambitions of his congregation to get on in this world.

"I have to believe a divine being created this world," she continued. "It is too interrelated to have happened by accident. But I can't be the kind of Christian my uncle is. I have to aggressively advance my people. That's my religion."

Dan Van Ness, the white student in the group, saw Christianity in a different light.

The son of a publishing executive, he had served as president of the student body at his large suburban high school before going on to Wheaton College. At graduation he was unsure of his life's direction and uncertain of his role in the organized church. Instead of enrolling in graduate school, as he had once planned, he took a year off to work with poor whites in the Chicago Uptown neighborhood. During this year he dropped out of church activities and read and thought about God's will for his life.

The next year he entered DePaul Law School, moved to the west side, and became active in Circle Church. Through Circle and socially concerned students at DePaul he learned about LaSalle's Legal Aid Clinic.

"My early church experience led me into a relationship with God," he confided to Chuck. "But it was very individualistic. An understanding of how I should relate to the needs of people came later. Now I'm discovering in Scripture that God wants us to be servants, which means living among the people we're trying to serve, seeking to understand the way they feel about life, helping them, and letting them help us.''

Six months later Dan Van Ness graduated from law school and took his bar exams. In the fall of 1975 he became Chuck's associate, working four days a week with LaSalle's Cabrini-Green Legal Aid Clinic and one day on the west side. The understanding was that when his year's apprenticeship was up, he would open a full-time clinic on the west side in conjunction with Circle Church.

Naturally Chuck was delighted.

Mind Food

13

Mind Food

THE SHIFTS AND CHANGES in programs at LaSalle during the late '60s and early '70s were enough to drive a traditionalist into future shock. Visitors returning to the church after a four- or five-year absence were bewildered. Only the weather-beaten sandstone church seemed to stay the same.

Bill Leslie was given to saying, "The church is for people, not programs: ministry to the present, not the past. When an activity becomes ineffective, it's time to make changes or cut it off. When circumstances force us to stop, we should look to see what God is teaching us. Sometimes it's necessary to take one step backward before we can take two steps forward."

The ill-fated coffeehouses were good examples. Growing violence had forced termination of The Extension. A famine of finances had shut down the Yellow House. Hostile young radicals had torpedoed Rahab's.

Evangelical backers had started pulling away months before Rahab's was closed. In the last weeks only a few diehards were still hanging on, and by the time the door was locked for the last time most had left for coffeehouse gambits in safer parts.

One of the few who hung around was Stan Shank, a bearded graduate of Wheaton, born in Gabon, Africa, of missionary parents.

Newly married and lacking only his thesis for his graduate degree in theology at Trinity Evangelical Divinity School, Stan felt there should be a continuing follow-up of contacts made through Rahab's and the two coffeehouses LaSalle had sponsored.

Stan knew his way around in counterculture circles. At Wheaton he had actively supported the anti-war candidacy of McCarthy, while rejecting the radical aberrations of the New Left movement. At the Democratic Convention Stan was disillusioned to see the political force of the student protest movement fizzle to nothing but street theater. He felt it would inevitably die from attrition.

After the Democratic Convention he enrolled at Trinity, channeled his extracurricular energies into Christian work, and managed Rahab's one night a week. With the forced closing of Rahab's two years later, two months after the student uprising against American intervention in Cambodia, Stan sensed that the activist spirit was fading fast. Walking the streets near his apartment, he would run into old acquaintances and ask them what they were doing. "I'm married and working to earn bread," some would say. More frequently, the reply was, "I've given up trying to beat the system. I'm into Eastern religions and learning some things about myself."

Stan and his wife Carol now lived in the Lincoln Park neighborhood about a mile and a half north of LaSalle Street Church. They had previously been attending Circle but had switched to LaSalle for its proximity to the north-side youth scene. Stan was wary of any outside organization's trying to send in a program for evangelizing the young adults on the street. He felt that the local church should meet the challenge in extending its ministry of outreach to the surrounding community.

One day he stopped by the church to talk with Bill Leslie. Their conversation quickly moved to mutual concerns.

"I think the coffeehouse thing with entertainment has had it around here," Bill said candidly. "It's an easy mark for troublemakers, and it costs too much to compete with other places. Also, I seriously doubt we could raise the money to start something new. Now if it was self-supportive . . . "

"Maybe a little store to sell used books and records, and two or three tables for serving coffee," Stan ventured.

Bill's eyebrows lifted a little. "Yeah, maybe. Come and make an announcement in our Fellowship Hour Sunday, and we'll see who might be interested. That's the way we work. Sound out people, and if they respond, then give them some handles."

Stan's suggestion was received with enthusiasm. One of the most eager to help was David Surbaugh, a lanky West Virginian and recent graduate of Trinity College. Stan, Dave, and about a dozen others began meeting on a weekly basis to pray and plan for the realization of a bookstore ministry.

Over a period of several months interest grew. "Little Al" Tamener, a well-known Hebrew-Christian record dealer, offered a thousand dollars of discs "to start you off." A literary-minded La-Saller thought "Middle Earth," the mythical land in J. R. R. Tolkien's trilogy, would be a good name.

Stan went to see Jim Johnson about generating some seed cash in Wheaton for rent and a stock of used books. Johnson, who continued as director of Evangelical Literature Overseas, told Stan, "You guys are thinking too small. If you want to become self-supporting, start a first-class bookstore. Sell Christian books and also secular titles to bring in non-Christians. Have a room in back for coffee and discussions."

Stan's eyes widened. "We hadn't been thinking in terms of acquiring that kind of capital."

"Well, think bigger, and I'll try to scare up some money in the book trade."

While Johnson talked to Christian publishers, Stan and Bill Leslie met with the LaSalle board. The board members were in favor of a bookstore but hesitant to commit the church to a property lease and an investment of several thousand dollars. They finally proposed that the business be set up as a separate entity. LaSalle members would help in the store, and some could serve with outsiders such as Jim Johnson on the board. The church would not be financially liable.

Johnson garnered pledges amounting to $5,000 from three Evangelical publishers and the Christian Booksellers Association. He recommended that Stan check on the possibility of becoming franchised with the Logos Bookstores, then a subsidiary of Inter-Varsity Christian Fellowship. Logos stores were situated near university campuses and doing well with books that appealed to young intellectuals. He felt the philosophy of Logos would be applicable to Chicago's north side.

Jim Carlson, head of the Logos stores, met with the planning group at the Leslies'. The franchise fee seemed reasonable in exchange for expertise in building inventory, setting up books and displays, and attracting business. The store would, of course, go under the Logos name.

The big hitch was additional money. At least $10,000 more was needed to meet franchise requirements for fixtures and stock. The Tyndale Foundation came through again.

The bookstore board leased a narrow 1300-square-foot building at 2616 N. Clark Street, near the Biograph Theater where John Dillinger had been shot. Space in the back was partitioned off for a children's bookshop, discussion room, and art gallery. The store staff planned for outdoor art shows in the long alley beside the store.

An eye-catching variety of greeting cards—religious, romantic, humorous, and funky pop art—were displayed on racks at the front. Logos had learned that many customers would stop in just to buy cards and other small items and stay to browse among the bookshelves.

The books were organized under catchy headings such as "Creative Brooding," "Know Thyself," and "The God Who Is There." Books with contrasting views on the same subject were placed together. A customer, for example, could come in for the autobiography of Malcolm X and notice the book next to it, Tom Skinner's *Black and Free*. The clerk could ask, "Have you read the story of this black revolutionary? He has something to say that's different from Malcolm X."

Stan Shank and Dave Surbaugh, the co-managers, became the full-time staff. Volunteers came in to help during rush periods.

Business was brisk from the time the store opened in May, 1972. An impressive 90 percent of customers during the first few months were estimated to be non-Evangelicals. This meant that some authors popular among Evangelical readers, such as Billy Graham, Corrie ten Boom, Keith Miller, and Eugenia Price, didn't sell as well as C. S. Lewis, Francis Schaeffer, John Powell, and others more appealing to young intellectuals.

Besides a ministry of "conversations" with customers, the store sponsored frequent discussions led by Christian authors, teachers, and other intellectuals. The discussions took place in the carpeted back room, with coffee and cookies served at the beginning.

In choosing discussion leaders and themes the staff first tried to be sensitive to topics of current interest. Second, they sought to slant discussions toward one of the three major groups the store was trying to reach: (1) secular, issue-oriented residents; (2) liberal social activists with some religious interest; and (3) Evangelically oriented persons, including Catholic charismatics.

Discussion leaders Kenneth Taylor and Joe Bayly drew a majority of Evangelicals. But when InterVarsity Press editor Jim Sire came to talk about the writings of Carlos Castaneda (an author offering mystical experience through drug use and contact with occult phenomena), there was only one Christian among the 29 present.

Discussions were well advertised. Ads were placed in the local underground "free" newspaper. Fliers and posters were put in neighborhood restaurants and bars that would accept them. But the best publicity channel was the store's quarterly newsletter, the *Apocalypse*, which soon had a mailing list of 1,800, many of whom were non-Christians.

By the second year of operation the store had become well known in the neighborhood. The north-side underground free paper ran an interesting review from its own perspective:

> Amid crosses and cards and posters with uplifting messages are titles like, *My Wife Made Me a Polygamist* and *International Cookbook*. Rather than humping for a particular sect, the owners have set a humanistic tone . . . .
>
> There's a potpourri of religious and philosophical titles,

181

> philosophy, poetry by Yevtushenko and extravagant artwork by Dali. Books at all prices, nothing used. Books are classed under headings like "The Greening of the Church," "Creative Broodings" and "Classical Literature Soul" (it doesn't really go back to the classics).
>
> A back room holds an exhibit by Moody Church Day Care students, and pottery, sculpture and paintings by local artists. There are even couches. Isn't that a novel idea, a bookstore with a place to sit?
>
> Serious, in-depth students of any particular novelist or type of work won't get very far here, but come in for the hell of it.

In addition to the discussions in the building, the bookstore sponsored a Saturday seminar for Christian writers at nearby McCormick Seminary. Jim Johnson headed a faculty of writers and publishers.

In each year of operation the store showed a modest financial gain. By 1975 the hope that outside supplements would no longer be needed seemed within reach. By this time there were volunteer workers who had been introduced to Christ through the store's ministry. These and other new believers participated in a Tuesday night Bible study and were also involved at LaSalle and other churches.

The biggest serious problem had been robberies. Twice, to Stan and Dave's chagrin, the bank deposit was grabbed by a "customer" who ran out of the store and got away before they could stop him. Fortunately, the checks from one deposit were returned by a taxi driver two months later. He had found them stuffed under the back seat of his cab.

The third robber was a bit more scary. A well-dressed man came in just before closing, browsed around until the regular customers had cleared out, then pulled a gun on a volunteer and left with the money.

The first two robberies taught Stan and Dave not to be so trusting. The third was part of the risk of operating a store in a crowded urban area.

In the last two years the bookstore has seen the Lincoln Park community around it change from a counterculture dominated by political activism to a society concerned with personal security and experiments in mysticism. As its audience has changed, the store has been able to be more flexible in creating an atmosphere for personal conversation. Furthermore, from the initial vision for a coffeehouse with books, the store has become a major resource in Chicago for both the secular and Christian community to explore and interact about the possibilities of Christian ministry and personal fulfillment. And as it has grown to reflect the larger church community, it has fed ideas back to LaSalle Street Church for an ever-broadening ministry.

Christian Counseling

14

Christian Counseling

THE LATIN *ne plus ultra* ("no more beyond") could not have been engraved on LaSalle Street Church. There was "more beyond" the weatherworn doors of the old sanctuary—much more than tutoring, community housing, legal aid, and an innovative bookstore. There was also the Near North Counseling Center, another first for an Evangelical church in the Chicago area, and one of only a few sponsored by local churches in the nation. Like other LaSalle programs, counseling came in response to growing awareness of human needs that were not being met elsewhere.

Many LaSallers came from churches which assumed that mental and emotional problems were the result of sin and disobedience to God. "You don't need a psychiatrist," preachers taught from their pulpits. "Read your Bible. Confess your sin and turn your life over to God. He is the answer for every problem."

Emotions were given little importance. Doubts, feelings of inadequacy, temper tantrums, hostility, and other interpersonal conflicts were to be confessed in a spirit of repentance. Related and deeper problems such as suicidal depression, frigidity, schizophrenia, paranoia, and delusions of grandeur went unrecognized.

By the 1960s a new day was breaking. Respectable leaders and institutions were cracking the silence and dishonesty of the past.

Psychologists Clyde Narramore and Henry Brandt got Evangelicals talking about the relationship between spiritual and mental health. In 1965 Fuller (Seminary) School of Psychology was established to train counselors and researchers. Suddenly it became known that other Evangelical schools were concerning themselves with mental health.

In that same year Keith Miller's *The Taste of New Wine* brought a new realism. At a time when young Evangelicals at LaSalle and elsewhere were becoming nauseated by phoniness and hypocrisy, Miller stripped away the facades. As much as anyone else in the '60s, "honest" Keith Miller made sin contemporary and redemption relevant to Christian living.

Through the '60s, LaSalle drew a steady stream of young fundamentalists with emotional and relational problems. They came because of LaSalle's reputation for honesty and acceptance. Here they could be themselves and share their anxieties and ambivalent feelings without fear of being put down.

Bill Leslie was sympathetic and approachable. While he had not been trained in counseling, he knew enough to recognize when professional help was needed. Arthur Volle was better qualified in the field, but at most he could give only a few hours each week.

In his daily counseling of Wheaton College students, he had become aware of the apathy, and in some cases coldness and harshness, of many home pastors toward youth with frustrations and inner conflicts. For instance, one of his counselees returned from Christmas vacation in emotional shambles. "I'm looked upon as a youth leader in our church," he said. "When I went home the pastor asked me to speak. I told him I was working through some doubts and personal problems and asked for a rain check. I thought he would be understanding. Instead, he blasted me for straying from the Lord."

Arthur Volle and Bill Leslie frequently talked about a full-time counselor at LaSalle, someone who could help individuals with deep-seated problems.

One day the Wheaton counselor came to Bill with a gleam in his eye. "You know we've been sending our emotionally disturbed students to the North Park Clinic. An intern there named Earl Laman has had phenomenal success with some of our kids. Their problems are about the same as what we see here at LaSalle.''

"Could he be a possibility for us?" Bill asked.

"Well, I thought we might set up a luncheon to get better acquainted.''

"Sure," Bill said. "Go ahead. I'll be there."

They met at the Town and Country Restaurant just off the Kennedy Expressway. Laman recalled his years as a Reformed Church in America pastor in Great Falls, Montana. ''I was confronted with all kinds of problems in my own life and in the church that the seminary never prepared me to handle. Without some good friends in the early years of my ministry, I don't know what would have happened. I went through a sorting-out period about what a church should be and what form my ministry should take. I concluded that a church should really take seriously its responsibility of caring for people.

"One morning a strange, disheveled, sallow-faced young man came to see me. I heard his story. When he was a baby, his father deserted his mother. A series of men came and went, and at 14 he left home. Some church people tried to help him, but he had so many problems they let him go back to the streets. At 16 he joined the Navy and found he didn't belong there. He got into trouble and went to jail where other prisoners abused him sexually. Back on the streets, he fell in with a cult. He left the cult in confusion, and met a girl who said she loved him. But when he went to see her she told him to get out or she'd call her father. After that he bummed around in bars awhile. Then he tried suicide and failed. A priest took him to the hospital where a Christian nursing aide suggested he see me.

"About all I could do was arrange for him to surrender to the military police. After he left I walked into the sanctuary and sat there looking at the big brown cross behind the pulpit. I thought of Christ and how He had dealt with people alienated from God; about how He said, 'Father, forgive them, for they know not what they do.' I felt that I and other pastors had been so intent on making people feel responsible and guilty for sin that we had missed the full implications of alienation.

"Well, it was this experience and others that propelled me to get special training. Now I feel God wants me to make counseling my full-time ministry."

They talked about Earl's immediate plans. He had had several offers from suburban churches. But he would give prayerful consideration to whatever might develop at LaSalle. "From what I hear you're my kind of church," he said.

Arrangements were made for Laman to speak at the Fellowship Hour—"so we can get better acquainted with you, and you with us," Bill said.

More discussions followed. A plan developed to rent offices near the church and charge a sliding fee of $10 to $25 an hour so counselees could pay according to their means. Those who could not meet the bottom figure would receive help from the church.

The Tyndale Foundation gave a starting grant of $5,000. Earl joined the LaSalle staff as director of the Near North Counseling Center in September, 1971. It was a step of faith for a father with four children, one of whom would be ready for college in a year.

Within six months he had a full case load of mostly young adults. Less than one in five came from LaSalle Church. By 1973 he needed help. Ka Tong Gaw, the former associate pastor at Circle Church, had experience in marriage counseling. He came to help part time. The following year Dave Bryen, an ex-Campus Crusade for Christ staff member and a graduate student in counseling at Trinity Divinity School, joined the center as an intern to work under Earl's supervision.

Many of the counselees had problems relating to their religious backgrounds. Harriet, for example, had been raised in the home of a strict fundamentalist minister. Then she was a dormitory assistant and an excellent student in Bible school. "I saw the world as very simple and dangerous," she told Earl. "It was out there. It didn't have anything to offer. I shouldn't get close to it or involved in it."

She had gone on to a Christian college for her degree. There she heard a different world view expressed by a psychology teacher. "He told us we would have to learn to live in the world. I didn't know how I

190

was going to fit. I began to feel that there was something wrong with me. I went into a depression.''

She bounded back and after graduation managed a thrift shop for a Jewish social agency. "Here I was in a different value system from what I had known. My associates thought differently. They drank wine—which I had been taught was evil—yet they seemed to enjoy happy, fulfilled lives and have wonderful family relationships. I had been taught that non-Christians were unhappy and frustrated and that secular work was strictly second-class with God. I stopped going to church. I lost interest in everyday things. I felt worthless.''

During a long series of weekly sessions Earl helped her discover the roots of her problem.

As a child, she had been repeatedly told that God was everything and she was nothing, that if she held to the right beliefs and suppressed wrong thoughts and feelings, a crown would be her reward. Consequently, she had choked off inclinations to be somebody and accomplish something in the world. Furthermore, she had denied the reality of her feelings of hatred, dislike, confusion, doubt, and sexual desire.

In the process, she had made her image of God like her authoritarian father. She had transferred her dependence on him to the Heavenly Father, looking for a blueprint of simplistic positives and negatives instead of following God in the adventure of growth and faith.

Having come to understand the deep-seated causes of her problems, she began building a more mature value system. Slowly, as confidence in herself as a worthwhile person and in God as a loving Heavenly Father grew, life took on new meaning.

Jill's problem was a bit more complicated. Coming from a strict fundamentalist upbringing in Iowa where "nobody had any fun," she had decided to live it up in Chicago.

She came to Earl in deep depression. Under his guidance, she soon became aware that guilt over a sexual liaison had pushed her into despondency.

"But I told myself sex wasn't wrong before marriage.''

"Uh huh," Earl replied. "But you couldn't erase the value system planted in your conscience." Over a period of time he helped her find forgiveness and see that God purposed only the best for His children.

George, a young Ohioan in his early 20s, had not thrown over his value system, but he complained of "feeling miserable."

"I think everything got converted except my feelings," he said. "I'm behaving, but I'm not enjoying it."

Exploratory questioning brought out that George's theology taught that all anger was sin and so he had suppressed it. "You didn't get rid of your angry feelings," Earl pointed out. "They've remained below the surface all the time. You'll have to bring them out and let God heal you." It turned out that, among other things, George had resented the career his parents had set for him, but he had never been willing to admit it.

In addition to counseling troubled singles, the Counseling Center became involved with marriage and family relationships. From 1973 on Earl was seeing persons who had sat under the teaching of Bill Gothard. The 29-year-old bachelor's Institute of Basic Youth Conflicts was becoming a phenomenon. In 1974, it was estimated, 250,000 paid an average of $35 each to hear 32 hours of counsel in mass meetings. Evangelical opinion on Gothard's teaching that the Bible has specific answers to every problem of life ranged from enthusiastic praise to caustic charges that he was misapplying and misinterpreting Scripture and spinning a web of legalism.

Listening to Gothard alumni, Earl saw both good and bad effects. Some with a low self-image of themselves were growing in healthy self-esteem. Some were building better interpersonal relationships. On the other hand, the LaSalle counselor felt some Gothard devotees had become too dependent on the Institute's system and could be stricken with yet more guilt in trying to follow Gothard's prescriptions for righting previous wrongs.

An example of the latter was a young woman who came to Earl on the verge of attempting suicide. Following Gothard's instruction to be in subjection to her parents in all things, she had gone to her father and confessed long-held bitterness. But instead of being understanding and forgiving, as she had expected, he had remarked sarcastically,

"Well, it's about time." The words had devastated her. She was so distraught that Earl had to refer her to a Christian psychiatrist, who in turn had her admitted to a hospital.

Besides directing the counseling center, Earl became a valuable resource person at the church, preaching occasionally, leading small therapy groups, encouraging cell groups among the scattered members, and writing prayers of confession for the worship services.

In January, 1975, he and Dave Bryen began a "Special-Focus Therapy Group on Feeling Accepted by Oneself, Others, and God." The group was limited to 15 persons who paid a "commitment fee" from $10 to $30 (according to their financial situation) to participate in 16 weekly one-hour Sunday morning sessions.

Earl and his wife Char continue to be active in their own LaSalle cell group in the northwest suburb of Des Plaines. "God created us with the capacity to belong," he says. "Six of us have been together for a year and a half. It's one of the few places where I feel I really belong and can be myself."

Every Sunday the congregation joins in his printed prayer of confession, which is included in the order of service. The prayer for February 24, 1974, aptly reflects his ministry of counseling and the fellowship of healing and growth at LaSalle Street Church:

> Great God, we are Your people—how we struggle to make that real! We are people of truth—but we respect it too little, let it slip away too often, deceive ourselves and others. We are people with feelings—but we repress and deny them, misuse and misdirect them. We are people of strength—but we work for just "things," drain our energy on only ourselves, serve inadequate ends. We are people who can communicate—but we speak too harshly and thoughtlessly, let out what we really don't mean, hold back what is upbuilding and needed. We are people of Your Spirit—but we blunt Your penetrating power, and squelch Your renewing moves. Struggle with us, Our God, now and in daily ways. Amen.

"Unto the Least of These..."

15

"Unto the Least of These..."

WHAT LASALLE NEVER LACKED in the troubled '60s and challenging '70s were people with needs—within and without the congregation. Just as the squeaky wheel gets the oil, the group with the most vociferous spokesperson received attention. The young adults asked for aid in building interpersonal relationships and got small-group cells' Neighborhood black youth demanded—sometimes in disturbing ways—that the church help them and got recreational and educational programs. People with emotional and psychological problems requested therapeutic guidance and got the counseling center. This explains, in part, why a programmed ministry to senior citizens did not begin until 1970.

LaSalle was a two-thirds singles church in the '60s, but as they paired off, it became a two-thirds couples congregation in the '70s. The average age increased little. The Moberg study showed 61 percent to be under 25; 80 percent below 35. Past 35 the numbers progressively lessened. There were only 12 persons aged 45-64. (The Volles, Boardmans, and Powells were jestingly called the "senile set"!) And just three past 65 turned in questionnaires.

Yet it was a different story in the neighborhood. An estimated 38,000 people over 65 lived within walking distance or a short CTA bus ride from the church. Most resided in tiny, drafty apartments and cheap hotels, living off welfare and/or Social Security, emerging only

197

once or twice a week to buy groceries and conduct other essential business. When they did go out, they tended to walk straight ahead, eyes darting right and left and often looking back to see if they were being followed. The robbery rate was highest on the third of the month, the day when Social Security checks came in the mail.

The only public housing available for seniors in the LaSalle neighborhood was in two 15-story high rises called Flannery Apartments. Some seniors who lived outside had been on a Flannery waiting list for four years.

A few oldsters dropped in for the worship services. Every month or so the church office had a call from a welfare agency requesting a hospital visit. Occasionally came a request for a funeral.

Bill and Adrienne sometimes compared the neighborhood seniors with the elderly they had known in Pekin. There, most had lived with or close to their families and enjoyed warm, loving relationships. Here, few seemed to have any relatives or friends who cared. "We've got to have a ministry to them," Bill would say. But there never seemed to be time. And the seniors never demanded it.

In 1970 Carol Stine, newly graduated from MBI, organized a church task force for senior citizens. The task force inaugurated an early Sunday morning breakfast for them. Carol and other young LaSallers came at 7:30 a.m. to prepare nutritional bacon-and-eggs-and-orange-juice breakfasts. While the food was being readied, others drove to the Flannery Apartments and other stops to pick up the invited guests. A 15¢ donation was "suggested" so that those who could afford to pay might maintain their dignity.

After eating, everyone was introduced. Then following a period of hymn singing, Frank Miller, a retired business executive and one of the three over-65s in the church, gave a five-minute Bible study. Carol announced that the guests could go home immediately in the vans or stay for the worship service and be taken home later.

When Carol left to work with a family-planning clinic in Pennsylvania, Jan Erickson, the social worker intern, took over the breakfast. Weekdays she visited the elderly in their homes and was on call for special assistance. Every day was different: cashing a Social Security check for a 75-year-old black woman who had fallen and broken her hip, holding off an impatient landlord with an emergency check from the church, driving an elderly widow to the doctor, helping a great-grandmother through the welfare maze.

Thursday was Senior Citizens Day at the church. They came in the morning for crafts and games, and then, after a light lunch, enjoyed a field trip to a park, a museum, or some other attraction in the Chicago area.

After Jan completed her internship, Beverly Barr was assigned to direct this ministry. Bev, a graduate of Wisconsin State University, had been employed at a home for emotionally disturbed girls. In September, 1974, she took over Jan's responsibilities as the senior citizens' coordinator and social worker.

Bev had helped as a volunteer worker before. Now as the coordinator she quickly learned some new guidelines.

One, always preview audiovisuals. She regularly got free recreational and educational films from the Chicago Public Library for Thursday morning showings. She usually previewed them, but one morning she was so busy that the time slipped away. What could be harmful about a film titled "Walking"? she wondered and slipped the spool on the projector. She saw the title and the screen credits come on, then left the projector running to complete a kitchen chore. A moment later she heard titters and gasps. Thinking the mixed reaction strange, she ran to the kitchen door and peeked into the fellowship hall. The characters were "walking" in the nude.

Two, check out seat reservations at entertainment places. She learned this after accepting a stack of free circus tickets. The seats were at the very top of the bleachers. It was like Pike's Peak for some of the seniors. As they huffed and puffed up the long climb, Bev feared that any instant someone might tumble over with a heart attack or stroke. Fortunately, there were no casualties.

Three, never take anything for granted. One Thursday afternoon they went to the Fire Department Academy on the west side for a field trip. A uniformed captain gave them a tour, explaining that the Academy had been built on the site where Mrs. O'Leary's legendary cow was said to have kicked over a kerosene lantern and started the great Chicago fire on the evening of October 8, 1871. Then the captain prepared to demonstrate how modern fire fighters were trained to slide down poles.

"The cadet goes up these stairs," he said as his heels clicked up the steel steps. Behind him came perky 72-year-old Rose. The stairs seemed safe enough. No one paid any attention to her.

The captain stepped onto the platform at the top of the ramp. "The cadet reaches out his right arm. Like this—" and leaping out, he squeezed the pole and zipped to the bottom.

While eyes were still on the captain, the audience heard a squeal. "Whee! Here I come!" Down came Rose, her arm squeezing the pole just as the captain's had, and hitting the floor with a plop. Office personnel who had been watching through a window came rushing out. The shocked captain bent over her calling, "Are you all right, madam? Do you want me to call an ambulance?"

Rose merely grinned and got to her feet. "I'm OK," she said. "I just wanted to try that trick for myself."

Bev also found that the seniors varied greatly in temperament. Some, like Rose, were usually pleasant and didn't want to be any trouble. Others could be very demanding, such as Leonore. "Where were you, Beverly, when I called this morning?" she would say, as if Bev had nothing else to do but sit by the phone. And some could be childishly rude, as at a Sunday breakfast when Joe, a resident in a seedy hotel, refused to stop talking during the Bible study. A few more were worrisome complainers who practically fought for her attention. One aging white woman, bordering on the psychotic, told a visitor one Thursday morning, "If Bev doesn't stop and listen to me, I'm going to kill myself." Later as the group peered through the glass windows of the thousand-foot-high John Hancock Building Observatory, she declared morosely, "This would be a good place to die."

A newcomer to the group overheard the remark and voiced alarm. Bev shrugged. "She talks that way a lot. The poor dear is just trying to get attention, I think. At least I hope that's why. She really doesn't have anybody except us."

200

Bev saw many of the seniors two and three times a week and came to know them well. There was Basil, 80, who walked as erect as a 20-year-old. He was retired from Montgomery Ward where he had helped print catalogs for over 40 years. Basil's only relative, a brother, had died a few years back, and he now lived alone in a tiny hotel room.

And Katie, a precious black woman who lived in a well-furnished apartment in Flannery and had a celebrity millionaire grandson who was a music composer. Katie had a beautiful sense of humor. "The roaches, they ride up with us," she told Bev as they were going up in the elevator to her apartment one day. Another time she remarked, "I don't mind getting old, but I don't want to get 'funny' like him," and pointed to one of the street men who sat in a corner and talked to himself.

And Blanche, who never spoke of any of her relatives. "Don't you have someone, somewhere?" Bev asked when taking her home one afternoon. "Oh, sure," she replied. "A sister and a brother in Iowa. But we haven't been on speaking terms since Mama died in '35. Not even a Christmas card."

And Sarah, who spoke with polished diction and was descended from the Pilgrims' William Bradford. Sarah lived in a once-fashionable downtown hotel and frequently called Bev to take her to the hospital for treatment or to the grocery store. Bev noticed that she always put her groceries in a department-store shopping bag. When she asked why, Sarah explained, "I don't want anybody to know I'm cooking in my room."

And Winnie, who would come regularly for awhile, then be absent for several weeks. When asked what she had been doing, she would launch into a long, rambling monologue about faraway exotic places. But with all her assumed affluence, Winnie had to be kept away from the kitchen or she would fill her purse with food.

The senior citizen programs wouldn't have been possible without volunteer help. Laurel Leslie helped adult volunteers prepare Sunday breakfasts. The eggs were brought by Bob Moore from a friend's brooder house in a small town 56 miles south of Chicago. Bob, a black lay minister, worked at a factory in the town and was a regular weekend guest of LaSalle members Dick and Candace Harbaugh. After Frank Miller became ill in 1973, Bob led the early Sunday Bible study. Other help in 1974-1975 was given by four college students doing practical social work.

As the church social worker, Bev was handling welfare problems for other ages. It irritated her to hear an occasional visitor sound off on how welfare clients were ripping off the taxpayers. She would patiently point out how difficult it was for some deserving people to get welfare.

Her star example was Jenny, an illiterate, dark-haired thirtyish woman of Rumanian descent whose husband had deserted her, leaving her with four young children all below the age of eight.

Jenny was receiving $374 a month from Aid to Dependent Children when her checks were suddenly cut off. Her $125 monthly rent past due, she was threatened with eviction and came to the church seeking help.

Bev's first inquiry at the local public aid office on North Milwaukee Avenue took six hours. A clerk said an audit of records had disclosed Jenny to be ineligible because neither she nor her children had birth or baptismal certificates. "They should never have been put on the roll," the worker informed Bev. "Somebody goofed by not requiring proof of identity."

The clerk stepped aside to check regulations. "Don't you have any proof of birth?" Bev asked Jenny.

"No papers. Nothing. My children were delivered by midwives. Me, too. But you can swear that you've known me for a long time. They'll take your word."

"But I haven't known you, Jenny. We'll just have to try another way."

The clerk returned. "We might get her on general assistance as a single person living alone. But she'd be getting $70 a month less than before."

"Better than nothing," Bev conceded. "How long will this take?"

"About 90 days," the clerk replied matter-of-factly.

Bev almost exploded. "Ninety days! She and the kids will be out on the streets and starved to death by then. Can't you speed it up or hustle up some emergency aid?''

''We'll put a rush on her check. In the meantime we might get her a one-time food allowance. Bring her back next Friday.''

At the church Bev took a call from the landlord. ''Unless half of the rent is paid immediately,'' he demanded, ''I'll have to put her out. I've got to have the income.'' Bev took the $62.50 from the church's emergency fund.

The following Friday Bev took Jenny back to the welfare office. They took a number and waited three hours for an intake clerk to give them an appointment with a caseworker. It was for the next Thursday morning at 8:30.

The six days passed. Jenny's food was running out. The church emergency fund was depleted, and Bev didn't know what could be done if the food aid wasn't given. To make matters worse, Jenny had become distraught and had fallen down the steps and broken her glasses.

They went back to the welfare office and waited. Finally Bev said, ''I've got to run down to the church and supervise the seniors. I'll be back later.''

The caseworker they finally saw at 2:45 p.m. seemed ignorant of Jenny's problem. ''Call her old ADC caseworker,'' Bev finally suggested in exasperation. The caseworker called and turned back with a smile. ''I think we can speed things up. Come back next Thursday and the food voucher will be ready.''

Bev was fit to be tied. The day when she was needed so badly with the senior citizens had been half wasted.

Somehow Jenny and the children survived another week. This time Bev telephoned before leaving the senior citizens at the church.

''Come in tomorrow morning,'' the caseworker said briskly.

''Will I have to wait?'' Bev asked.

''No, it'll be ready.''

But they still had to wait an hour for the food voucher in the amount of $68.66.

Bev now drove Jenny over to Treasure Island, a well-stocked

supermarket in Old Town. They rolled a cart along the aisles, looking for the best buys. Bev tried to keep tabs of the prices. The voucher had to be spent completely. No change could be returned.

When Bev thought they were close to the goal, they got in line at a checkout counter. The cashier rang up the total. They were $15 short. Bev had to make three trips back while people behind waited impatiently.

Another week passed and still the $304 general assistance check had not come. The landlord called again. "I must have the other half of the month's rent," he insisted. "By tomorrow. No later."

Bev went to Bill in desperation. "We'll have to rob Peter to pay Paul and take it from the senior citizens' fund," he said. Once more the landlord was mollified.

Another week and no welfare check. Bev went to see Jenny and found a neighbor had been giving the family a little food.

Overtired, Bev had been feeling sorry for herself. Now her self-pity turned to anger at the slowness of the welfare bureaucracy. "How long, how long," she mumbled.

The check came. At last. Jenny could pay her rent, and when that $125 was subtracted she would have $179 left to care for herself and four children during the next month.

The weekly staff meeting was the next day. "Any victories to report?" Bill asked.

Bev raised her tired eyes. "Yeah, let's all praise the Lord. Jenny got her check."

Everyone cheered. They knew what Bev had been going through.

Bill looked around the table at which they sat in the fellowship hall. "The arrival of Jenny's check will never make a mark in this city's history," he said. "Nor will a thousand other things we do along this line. But the Lord keeps records a little differently."

The Beat Goes On

16

The Beat Goes On

ALL OF LASALLE'S FAITH-STRIDES in tutoring, cell groups, youth programs, housing, counseling, legal aid, and ministry to senior citizens came before the attempted robbery and beating of Bill Leslie.

As Bill lay bruised and battered while his assailants debated whether to finish him off, he could take comfort that he had led the church in good beginnings. If God allowed them to kill him, surely God would raise up another leader to carry on the work.

Then while he was still praying, he became aware that the church was silent. They had gone! He was alive!

He waited a minute or two to make sure they had indeed gone. Then he tried to wriggle his hands free of the ropes. Unable to do this, he managed to work the gag loose from his mouth and untie the belt that bound his feet. Still dazed, he stumbled into the office and called the police, then Dan Good and Dave Bryen. The staffers came on the run and untied his wrists. Police then arrived and took him to nearby Henrotin Hospital where he spent the afternoon in the emergency and X-ray rooms. Except for bad gashes above one eye which was closed, wounds across the top of his head and under his chin, bruises about his body, and a painfully sore stomach, he was OK. His assailants were never apprehended.

The following Sunday Bill candidly described his frightening experience. "I think it would be better if we close the books on this. It might be good for fund-raising, but it will keep some people from coming to our church.''

In August, 1975, Bill finally handed in his doctoral dissertation—''The Status and Role of Women in the Pauline Churches in Light of the Social and Religious Environment of the First Century.'' This marked the end of 14 years of graduate study. Earlier he was cited at Wheaton College's commencement for ''pioneering numerous innovative programs aimed at inner-city problems.'' He was also one of six Wheaton alumni named to Wheaton's Scholastic Honor Society.

The Leslies continue living on Crilly Court. Laurel and Lisa are in the 11th and 9th grades, respectively. Laurel has been chosen to be piano accompanist for the Chicago Youth Symphony Orchestra. Andy, a promising young violinist, is in third grade, and little Scott attends the Moody Church Day Care Center. To keep them in private schools, Adrienne teaches art at the Communications Art Center at the Walt Disney Magnet School.

The house is delightfully decorated with Adrienne's abstract-expressionist paintings. The living room is an airy white and flows past a fireplace into the dining area. The spaciousness of the first floor area is important. At times they entertain over 100 people.

The shadow of crime has lengthened over the neighborhood. Doors must be locked at all times. Everything of value must be kept inside the house. The total number of bikes stolen from the Leslies is now seven.

Crime is something LaSallers have learned to live with. Chuck's legal aid office has been burglarized. Intruders broke into the church while people were meeting in the fellowship hall and took cleaning equipment. As a diversionary tactic they emptied a wastebasket in the men's room and started a fire. By the time the fire was discovered the ceiling and walls of the men's room were charred. Had not the heat cracked the toilet bowl, releasing a stream of water, fire might have engulfed the building. ''God was really with you,'' a fire fighter declared.

Many LaSalle members have had their apartments burglarized. A number have joined the company of the mugged. Thankfully, none have suffered serious injury.

Ron Cook, the former assistant pastor, now manages a Logos bookstore in Champaign, Illinois. Jim Backstrom, a Wheaton grad in sociology, is the new pastoral assistant. He coordinates cell groups, hospitality, visitation, Friday night get-togethers for singles, and the discipling of new Christians.

Dan Good works part time while studying for his master's at the Jane Addams School of Social Work. Having completed his seminary work, Dave Bryen is a full associate in counseling to Earl Laman. He also attends the Family Institute of Chicago. They would like to add another counselor. Cathy Biddinger, another Wheaton grad, doubles as secretary for both the counseling center and the church.

Besides directing activities for senior citizens and handling special welfare problems, Bev Barr also heads up the weekday girls' clubs. Omer Reese still directs the music program.

Three new interns make additional outreach possible. Gracia Tan Hee, a native of Singapore, coordinates work with internationals. June Dorn assists Bev Barr with senior citizens. Dave Mack, a Young Lifer coaching at a neighborhood school, is involved with high school boys. The church plans to hire a black to work alongside Dave.

Chuck Hogren, his new associate Dan Van Ness, and the clinic's new office manager, Lynette Surbaugh (Gina Berg resigned to await the birth of her first child), find there is not enough time for all the legal aid requests they receive.

Stan Shank and Dave Surbaugh remain with the Logos bookstore.

The counseling center and the bookstore are more financially secure than the legal aid clinic, which continues on the edge of a fiscal cliff. One church leader in Wheaton, after hearing a legal aid presentation, wondered why Chuck couldn't go back to his old practice and do charity work part time. The uncertain financial picture makes it difficult to plan ahead. But a recent grant from the Illinois Humane Society will keep legal aid going another year, and a $1,000 typewriter donated by the Northside Kiwanis Club speeds office work.

The newest staff member is Judie McAndrews (nee Hultman), a former professor of education at Northeastern Illinois University, who heads the expanded tutoring program. One-on-one tutoring by volunteers has been expanded to Monday and Tuesday evenings at the church and two afternoons each week at the Franklin School behind the church. With Franklin having one of the lowest reading scores in the city, the concerned principal was happy to accept La-Salle's offer of help.

Though new people keep arriving, LaSalle's membership has become a little more stable. All of the Wheaton "short termers" are still at the church. A number of talented young professionals, both singles and couples—some of whom met at the church—have become "fixtures" (three years of participation).

Dozens of occupational specialties are represented among La-Sallers. As might be expected, the helping and teaching professions have the largest representation. Doctors, lawyers, teachers—some of whom serve in schools where police officers patrol the halls—and social workers rank high.

The creative arts are well represented also. Stuart Carlson, for example, teaches art at North Park College. "I was never asked to have an art exhibit in churches I attended before. I wasn't here more than two months when Bill asked for a display of my paintings on the theme of rebirth. They were used in connection with a sermon series."

LaSallers serve outside the church in creative, meaningful ways. Lois Ottaway, for instance, was voted PACE's "Volunteer of the Year" for her service in the inmate rehabilitation and training program at the Cook County Jail. Don and Betty Boardman work with Project Hope, a Catholic organization that helps poor people rehabilitate run-down houses in the suburbs. Before going to Pakistan for a year of university teaching as a Fulbright professor, Don served as president of the Wheaton School Board.

But for everyone, Sunday in the beloved old sanctuary at LaSalle and Elm is the highpoint of the week. Take one typical Sunday in 1975:

8:00 a.m.: You can smell the bacon frying for the senior citizens' breakfast.

8:10: The senior citizens are arriving. "How're you feeling, Maude?" Bev asks a stooped black woman. "Tolerable, just tolerable. My arthritis was acting up this morning. But once I got out of bed, I was OK. I'll live to praise the Lord.''

8:15: The old folks are in line to be served. For many this breakfast and the Thursday lunch will be the most nutritious meals they will eat all week. They carry their paper plates to round tables, covered today with red and white checkered cloths, and join in animated, friendly conversation.

8:40: "Let's everybody sing," Bob Moore announces. Laurel Leslie is at the piano. "Uhhhmazin' Graaace, how sweeeet the soundddd.'' They sing slowly, relishing each syllable, some following behind others, some voices still remarkably clear, some creaky and raspy. Basil, ramrod straight, sits next to a one-armed man with hair askew. Next to him is an aged Filipino. In the corner a little Caucasian with a blue bandanna wrapped around his head talks to himself. A black woman, wearing a feathered hat, frowns at him.

8:55: With his tie loosened, and walking among the tables as he talks, Bob Moore is giving his sermonette. "Paul didn't fear to speak for Jesus. No, indeed. Not even when he stood before King Agrippa. And, friends, we oughtn't be afraid either to let our friends know that we love the Lord.''

9:00: Bob winds up his short message. He knows the old folks have short attention spans. Now everyone can hear clearly Omer Reese's small choir rehearsing in the back room.

The choir has five men and five women. Three men have beards. Two of the women wear long dresses. The remaining three are in jeans. Eyes are fixed on the director. "One-two-three-four-five-six," he beats. "Ooh—ooh—doo—doo—doo. OK, let's do it. 'Come, let us to the Lord return . . . .' ''

9:45: Candles are lit on the sanctuary altar. A white-headed man checks hymn racks to see that no books are missing. Organist Anita Smith plays a soft prelude. Four ushers—two men and two women— hand bulletins to early arrivals. Anita continues the organ meditation as the gathering people reflect on the printed prayer of preparation: "Here I am again, Lord, needing to meet You, the Living God, and to be changed by that meeting."

211

10:00: About 250 are in the sanctuary, with some stragglers coming in. Robert Allen, a tall, balding salesperson for a steel company, who is new to the church, reads the call to worship from Psalm 32. After a hymn of praise, "We Come, O Christ, to Thee," Martha Kerr, a former intern, gives the invocation.

From the rear balcony the choir sings its anthem.

Jim Backstrom, wearing a red-striped polo shirt and slacks, gives the prayer of intercession:

> We bring our needs before You, Lord, because we believe You care and will answer. We pray that You will relieve the pains of those who are aching and that You will show us Your goodness and love.
>
> We pray for families who have lost husbands, for policemen who have been shot, and for families of those who have been shot by police. We pray for the leaders of our country, although we have questions about some of them. We pray for the suffering peoples of Cambodia and Vietnam. We pray for those who are Your people there. Help them find hope in Thee.

The congregation sings the Hymn of Prayer, "Jesus, Thou Joy." Children through sixth grade leave for their Sunday school classes downstairs.

Jim welcomes visitors and makes necessary announcements. The ushers pass offering plates. Dave Bryen and Dan Good, both in informal garb and each speaking from a pulpit, lead the responsive Scripture reading from Romans. The emphasis is on God's acceptance of those who trust in Christ.

Earl Laman rises to give the sermon. (Bill is taking a month's leave of absence to complete his doctoral dissertation.) A month ago Earl spoke on alienation—how sin, individually and collectively, alienates persons from God and one another. Today his subject is acceptance—how the faith-salvation relationship opens up acceptance on both the horizontal and the vertical planes. Some samplings:

> By our faith we are ushered into a new relationship—a new bond that can heal the breach and close the alienation gap. . . . God took

the initiative to us. He is seeking to bridge the gap. He is saying, "You are lost. I want to find you. I want to come into relationship with you."

All kinds of people came to Jesus—lepers, tax collectors, harlots. He accepted them. As we accept His love, His acceptance of us becomes real power that is let loose among us.

Acceptance is one of the strong forces in this church. A lot of us are still in transition, still questioning, still searching, but while we struggle, we find acceptance. That acceptance is just as real in tutoring, counseling, legal aid, the bookstore and other manifestations of the Gospel.

Acceptance stands in stark contrast to guilt as preached in many churches who say people must be made to feel rotten before they can embrace God. I am not talking about real guilt, of course, but the way guilt is used. . . . Look how Jesus related to the woman at the well. No rejection. No put down. Just acceptance.

I remember a young woman who came to LaSalle from a rigid background. Her austere, autocratic father had colored the face of God. She made some very sarcastic statements at Fellowship Hour, about how she could not accept some of the things we were doing. Yet afterwards four people walked up and said in various ways, "I accept you." As she kept coming back, she received more acceptance, and finally she came to the counseling office. There as we talked together, she began to open and really admit what went on inside her. She came to accept herself as she really was and to know that God accepted her. She came to accept others as full brothers and sisters in Christ.

Acceptance is the key. It opens up new working relationships for renewal and dealing with faults. I've seen it happen so many times in marriage, partners accept each other's foibles and feelings . . . and in the church family, too.

Have you really looked at the acceptance which God has provided you in Christ? I can promise that it will open a working relationship in which all kinds of things are possible.

213

Earl concludes his sermon and the congregation joins in a Prayer of Confession:

> Living Lord, You have revealed so much to us. We know so much that was hidden and unfathomable. But we must confess that there is often such a discrepancy between what we know and what we do with it. We claim to know You but forget there is so much more to understand; we know you are preparing us for greater living but we expect too little; we know enough to see and hate all that is destructive but we don't get upset enough to act; we know others need our support but we hold back. We know we have much to share but we hang on to it; but we also know that Your pardon and understanding and loving help are real, so we turn to You silently now . . .

Dave Bryen speaks again: "You are invited to celebrate the assurance of your acceptance. Let this be a special celebration." The choir sings, then Dave leads the Litany of the Bread:

> MINISTER: Even as grain of the Earth grows richly across broad plains,
>
> PEOPLE: And is piled high in lofty elevators, and baked into millions of loaves daily,
>
> MINISTER: So great, O God, is the storehouse of Your acceptance for the people of Your world;
>
> PEOPLE: So great, O God, is the storehouse of Your acceptance that has come to us;
>
> MINISTER: Take, eat, God's acceptance of you is as real as the bread you take into your hands;
>
> PEOPLE: I will take and eat; God's acceptance of me is as real as the bread I take into my body.

The bread is served by two men and two women.

Earl walks to the center of the altar-platform and turns to face the audience. "Accepted by Him, take, eat."

A couple, Rich and Nancy Ball, give a dramatic reading from I Corinthians 5:16-19 and Galatians 3:26-28 about faith, forgiveness, acceptance, and the union of believers in Christ. As they speak, Rich softly strums his guitar.

Dave directs the Litany of the Fruit of the Vine:

MINISTER: Even as the vineyards stretch across a thousand valleys,

PEOPLE: And as the juices are taken from the shelves of tens of thousands of stores,

MINISTER: So great, O God, is the reservoir of Your acceptance for the people of Your world;

PEOPLE: So great, O God, is the reservoir of Your acceptance that has reached us;

MINISTER: Drink of it; God's acceptance of you is as personal as the shimmering cup you hold in your hand;

PEOPLE: I will drink of it; God's acceptance of me is as personal as the flavor I taste.

Earl again faces the congregation and holds up his cup. "It is for you. Drink it."

The Balls present a second dramatic reading of Scripture from Romans 8 to guitar accompaniment:

All join in "An Expression of Acceptance":

I believe in the forgiveness of sins . . .

    for bus drivers who grunt and curse
    for gang leaders who bring fear and intimidation
    for politicians who love power and their friends
    for religious people who are insensitive and
        judgmental
    for officials who won't see people's needs
    for parents who don't understand and won't listen
    for real estate promoters who call on the telephone
    for fellow workers who make the job tougher
    for clerks who could care less
    for businessmen who have shoddy ethics
    for drivers who cut in
    for policemen who extort
    for reacting teenagers
    for relatives who reject
    for friends who gossip
    for pimps and pushers
    for people who can't forgive
    for church leaders

215

for arsonists
for athletes
for rich people
for weirdos
for my kids
for you
for me.

The congregation joins in a hymn of celebration, "Joyful, We Adore Thee," then the service is concluded with a benedictory song-prayer by soloist Carol Metzger.

11:00: People are crowding into the fellowship hall, picking up cookies and Styrofoam cups of coffee and tea, calling to friends, slipping into seats around the tables.

11:10: Jim Backstrom introduces first-timers. Announcements are made from the floor. Needs are expressed. Responses are given to meet the needs.

11:20: Earl is the program for today's Fellowship Hour. He invites questions and comments about his sermon on acceptance.

Madelyn Powell: "Is acceptance the ultimate we get from God?"

Earl: "No, it's only the entrance into relationship."

Madelyn: "But are acceptance and forgiveness the same? What about repentance? To be forgiven you must realize you're a sinner, recognize your guilt, repent and ask for forgiveness. The prodigal son said, 'Father, I have sinned against God.' "

Earl: "I agree, but you should feel real guilt, not the false guilt that some churches push on people."

The exchange continues between Madelyn and Earl. Each tries to understand the other as they touch on matters which theologians have worried over for centuries.

The subject shifts. Instead of replying to a question, Earl asks, "Anybody here who'd like to try and answer that?" The time passes too quickly. Too many questions are left unraised, many ideas left unspoken.

This Sunday evening there will be two forums at the church: a study

216

of Psalms, led by Madelyn; and a critique of Bill Gothard's Seminar on Basic Youth Conflicts, led by Dave Bryen. Future Sunday evenings will offer different activities. Volleyball on the beach. An open house at someone's apartment where people may come and go as they wish. An ice-cream social with discussion to follow.

Some upcoming weekday activities are a square dance in the fellowship hall for the "Duos" (married couples) and a picnic at the Indiana Dunes for the "Unos" (singles).

Monday afternoon is girls' club at the church. Monday evening, tutoring.

Tuesday morning the staff comes to the fellowship hall for their weekly breakfast meeting. Bill takes time off from his dissertation to preside. On the agenda are reports, assignments, and ten "general matters" to discuss (for example a food co-op, a retreat, and a church family banquet).

The beat goes on. Chuck dashing about in his 1970 Volvo, trying to make four court appearances at four different locations in one day. Stan and Dave rapping with a Satan worshiper at the bookstore. Bev and a crew of volunteers escorting a group of senior citizens to the Museum of Science and Industry. Dan Good taking his boys' club swimming. Cells all during the week from Evanston in the north to the Hyde Park/University of Chicago area in the south.

Bill, John Petersen, and Chuck Hogren attend the monthly board meeting of the Chicago-Orleans Housing Corporation. Bill, still the chairperson of the consortium of church representatives, has good news to report: the $10 million loan is approved; they're almost ready to select the contractor; groundbreaking could come in a couple of months.

The LaSalle Street Church high rise for senior citizens—the building scheduled to have church facilities on the lower floors—is now a diminishing possibility because of the economic pinch. Recognizing this, the church has purchased an old house in back, along with three empty lots, for $50,000, which is being paid off under a three-year mortgage. Mobile classrooms are to be put on the lots, which, with the house, will provide badly needed space for the expansion of youth

217

programs. The real estate was purchased at an opportune time. Land prices are expected to double after construction of the Chicago-Orleans Housing Corporation's big development begins across Wells Street.

The old sanctuary is unlikely to be torn down. In 1975 it was designated a "landmark" of Chicago by a commission of architects and historians. Nor is it likely to undergo a complete renovation. The estimated cost for this was put at $300,000 in 1970.

It looks much the same. The stained-glass Good Shepherd still gazes down on busy LaSalle Street. Beneath the window, the heavy door bears more scars. The latch is shinier from the prying knife blades of would-be intruders. The lower concrete step is crusted with a gray patch of dried vomit where an inebriated passerby stopped the night before. Close examination of the sandstone reveals chipped spots where bullets ricocheted off during the 1968 battle between the National Guard and the rioters. The inscription on the cornerstone is faded, but you can still make out the inscription:

A MIGHTY FORTRESS IS OUR GOD

1882

LaSalle and Moody Church have worked to build new ties. The two youngest Leslie children have attended the Moody Day Care Center. Three of the Center's workers attend LaSalle. Dr. Dale Layman, a member of LaSalle, is on the board of the center. Moody Church has sent several people to Earl Laman for counseling and helped pay their fees.

"We had our problems, for which I was partly at fault," Bill admits. "I should have stayed in closer touch with the Moody Church board. I was wrong about that. While we still differ on some things, I think we all realize that we need each other in the body of Christ, and we realize that there should be a variety of types of ministries."

LaSalle and the Moody Bible Institute also enjoy a closer working relationship. MBI students are once again being encouraged to participate in LaSalle's outreach ministries. LaSalle has undoubtedly influenced changes at MBI; exactly how much is hard to determine.

MBI, for one thing, anticipates a new major course of study called American Intercultural Ministries in which students may train for specialized work among American Indians, blacks, Asians, the Spanish-speaking, and rural people. "We hope it will be a model for other Christian schools," one faculty member says.

"Chicago with its variety of ethnic groups is particularly fitting as a training ground for ministries to minorities," he notes. "Students will be assigned to work in churches that are already relating to these groups. LaSalle will likely be one of the first, and we expect close cooperation with Bill Leslie and his staff."

LaSalle is becoming better known across the country. Visitors keep popping up on Sunday to see what's happening. Bill Leslie, for one, is apprehensive about LaSalle becoming a show church. "What worked here may not work in other places. Besides, we have a long way to go."

LaSalle is still skating on thin ice financially. The congregational offerings are up—about $65,000 in 1974. But this was only 40 percent of the total spent on all ministries. The balance had to come from other churches and Christian foundations.

"The difficulty is getting money to sustain programs started several years ago," Bill says. "We have to face it: Evangelicals' interest in the inner city has waned. Yet the needs, even greater than they were in the '60s, are still here.

"We're constantly praying and looking for new ways to generate money. We keep hoping more churches will see that teaching kids to read, for example, is just as important here as in Africa or Asia, and will put us in their missionary budget. We've talked about starting a business, perhaps a cleaning establishment, that will provide some jobs and produce some money for our programs. We're open to the Lord's leading in any direction."

An internal concern relates to the requirements for membership. Presently, applicants must serve three months in a church ministry before becoming eligible to join the church. Some would like to make it harder to become and stay a member. A LaSalle delegation has visited the Church of the Savior in Washington, which requires a year or more of preliminary study and then a discipline of daily prayer and Scripture reading, faithful attendance at weekly worship, active membership in a mission group, and giving a tithe (at minimum) to the church. But the Church of the Savior is almost all middle-class and well-educated people, whereas LaSalle's membership scales from Ph.D.s to some who can hardly read or write. It would be hard, if not impossible, for all of LaSalle's people to meet the Church of the Savior's requirements.

Building a community of faith is a continuing struggle. Many of the married couples who were singles in the neighborhood during the '60s now have children. Several have moved to Evanston because of the good schools there, and they commute to the church. Some who do not have children cannot afford the high rents in the neighborhood. Bill is hopeful that a number of LaSalle people will move into the Chicago-Orleans Housing Corporation's development when it is open for residency (scheduled for 1977). "We're glad to have all our loyal commuters," he says, "but we can't have an impact on the community until a good percentage of us live here."

Safety remains critical. Hardly a month passes without someone in the church being robbed, either on the street or at home.

And because LaSalle is an open church (anyone can attend and speak at the monthly board meetings) there is continuing discussion—sometimes causing tension—on theological, social, and program issues.

"I look back and realize that we've only made it this far by the grace of God," Bill reflects. "I look ahead and wonder how we will keep going. All I can say for certain is that we'll keep striving to be God's ministering people."

220

APPENDIXES

Appendix A

CONSTITUTION OF LASALLE STREET CHURCH (SELECTED PORTIONS)

This church, as one unit in the larger Body of Christ, joins in the common purpose to be God's instrument in this world. As such, it is to provide both the opportunity and incentive for the worship of God, to proclaim the Good News of salvation in Jesus Christ, to foster maturity in believers, to provide loving fellowship for all, and to minister to the needs of the whole man.

Observing that liberal churches had become unbalanced in one direction and conservatives in another, the members of LaSalle formulated a doctrinal statement that emphasized both beliefs and relationships, faith and commitment, doctrine and ethics.

. . . Let it always be remembered that one may have right ideas about God and be in wrong relation to Him. A Christian is not simply an individual who has dedicated himself to a certain theological system of thought or a particular ethical code. A Christian is one who has responded with faith to God's saving act in Jesus and who has committed himself in personal trust and life venture to Him. Doctrine and ethics both play an essential role in the life of a Christian, however; doctrines describe the facts which men encounter in entering this life-giving relationship with Jesus Christ and one's behavior both follows from believing these truths and serves to maintain the vitality of the relationship. Without both, it is impossible to know the living God fully.

223

They cited the historic Apostles' Creed as the embodiment of "the cardinal and essential facts of the Christian faith," then expanded the famous statement of the Church fathers with eight affirmations—"to clearly chart our course through the present and confused theological milieu."

1. That the one living and true God, who created all, who upholds and governs all, and who is sovereign over the natural order and the affairs of men and who will bring all things to their conclusion according to His design, is personally and actively concerned about the well-being of all men. In demonstrating this concern, He has disclosed Himself simultaneously to man as the Father Almighty, as Jesus Christ our Lord, and as Holy Spirit, these eternally existent three being one God.

2. That Jesus Christ invites all men to a life-giving relationship with Himself. In the beginning He "was with God" and He "was God." Entering the human sphere, He "emptied Himself . . . being born in the likeness of men." Being truly and fully human, He endured all conditions common to man including temptation and suffering. He is therefore able to "sympathize with our weaknesses." As revealer, simultaneously He disclosed to man what God is like and what the characteristics of true humanity are in the purpose of God; but the human predicament demanded that Jesus be more than simply a revealer and example. Thus, Jesus, by His life of obedience, His death and His resurrection, made an atonement for sin, making it possible for all men to know God and to receive the gift of eternal life.

3. That the Holy Spirit is active both in the unbelieving world and in the lives of Christians. He works to bring men into relationship with God; and, subsequent to the believer's acceptance by God, He aids man as spiritual teacher, guide, and inner moral power. He also rules the Church by the Word of God.

4. That every man possesses intrinsic worth by virtue of his creation in the image of God. Man, however, created to live in a spiritual relationship with God and to glorify Him, fell into bondage to the powers of sin and death because of his willful estrangement from

224

God. Man's declaration of independence from God, his sinful attitudes and acts, have brought a blight to human life and a sense of unfulfillment.

5. That any man's relationship to God is restored by embracing Jesus Christ as his personal Lord and Savior. This is done through faith alone, which consists of a humble acceptance of what God has done for man through Jesus Christ, a willingness to be a mere receiver of this gift and nothing else, and a complete surrender of the whole personality to the influence of the risen Christ. The fruit of such faith invariably results in the discovery of true freedom, in a sense of wholeness and completeness, and in good works.

6. That each believer is an integral part of the local manifestation of the Body of Christ and has a responsibility to that body to exercise his gifts for its health, growth, and vitality. Further, the risen Lord gave two ordinances to His Body which are outward symbols of inward spiritual realities, baptism and the Lord's supper.

7. That history will culminate in the second coming of Jesus Christ. The unbelieving living and resurrected dead will account for the investment of their lives and will be sentenced to ultimate and eternal separation from God. Those who by faith in Jesus Christ have been accepted by God will give account of their stewardship since becoming believers and will share eternity with the Lord.

8. That the Bible is the record of God's revelation of Himself and His will for mankind. In it, God has revealed the provision He has made for man's salvation. It is an all-sufficient rule of belief and practice.

Government was vested in the membership with the elected church board "responsible for all functions and operations of the church." The old fundamentalist negatives against movies, dancing, card-playing, etc., were dropped. A membership applicant was to affirm "personal trust in Jesus Christ as Savior and Lord" and "agreement with the Articles of Faith," and to "commit his life to Jesus Christ in disciplined service in the church." A member could be dropped from the roll for inactivity or for "leading an unworthy life."

225

Appendix B

WORKING PAPER ON WORSHIP

In the narrowest sense, worship is the response of the total person (intellectual, emotional, and volitional or commitment-making part) to God in the ascription of praise to Him for who He is (characteristics or attributes) and what He has done (words, attitudes, and deeds). It is an emotional and committing response to an intellectual evaluation of God. As heroes call forth our admiration, praise, and enthusiasm in spontaneous response, so much more does God. The word used for worship means to crouch, to kiss, to do homage, to prostrate oneself, to reverence. Further, true worship always reaffirms previous commitments and makes new commitments based on the new understanding achieved in the service. These are the "gifts" of the Spirit to which Jesus referred when He said, "God is spirit, and those who worship him must worship in spirit and truth" (Jn. 4: 24, RSV)

In its broader sense, worship is the offering of any gift to God in love—a gift of the Spirit mentioned above, a material gift, or the gift of a deed, a relationship, or even a vocation if they are "in His name." This makes worship a life-style and transforms all the secular into the sacred.

In either case, the primary posture of the worshiper is giving. Worship essentially is *giving* rather than *getting*.

1. Worship is a direct dialogue between God and the congregation so the worship service should be structured on this basis rather than

the congregation and the minister talking to each other about the third person—God. This means the hymns used primarily should be those addressed to God as prayers (praise, thanksgiving, confession, consecration, petition, and intercession) rather than those addressed to our fellows (testimony and exhortation). Time also should be allotted for listening to God speak to us through Scripture, the sermon, the sharing of a fellow believer, and the quietness of meditation. Since true dialogue is two-way communication, time also must be allotted for our response to God in both structured and free prayer times.

Example: Litany: UNITY IN DIVERSITY

Leader: Our Father, here we are, having come from our private little worlds, feeling fragmented and alone.

People: Thank You for bringing us together anyway.

Leader: Our Father, some of us didn't feel like coming today because we thought no one really cared.

People: But You care. Thank You for caring.

Leader: Sometimes we've found it difficult to see anything of each other except our different shades of clothes and skins.

People: We're grateful Your vision isn't so superficial.

Leader: Lord, we've felt at times others haven't given us the respect we were entitled to because of our education or position.

People: Thank You for making us feel important by coming among us as an ordinary worker, a carpenter.

Leader: At times this past week we've scorned the failure of the weak and envied the success of the strong.

People: Remind us of the new understanding of failure and success brought us through the cross and the empty tomb.

Leader: As men, we fear our women want to take away our manhood; as women, we feel our men treat us as servants.

People: Lord God, You who have been a mother and a father to us, help us recognize each other's dignity as persons without denying each other's gifts as men and women.

228

Leader:	Some of us feel we're left out because we're young and wear long hair, and others of us, because we're old and obsolete.
People:	Eternal Christ, help us build bridges across the years that separate us.
Leader:	Young and old, men and women, black and white—in all our multitudinous variety we have come together today to worship You.
People:	Our Father, we thank You for all the richness of our colors and cultures. Help us to use our differences to enrich each other's lives. Help us to build Your kingdom out of our diversities.
Leader:	And so, as we pray the prayer Jesus taught His disciples, help us to recognize in it our common needs, our common resource, our common goal.
All:	(The Lord's Prayer)

2. Worship should be a joyous time and include much celebration as well as introspection and meditation. It should be impregnated with the robust expression of a people full of confidence in God and His creation, who marvel at the sheer abundance of His power.

Example: Several little girls ballet (dance) into center stage. Holding paper flowers, they squat low, holding their flowers in the center of their circle. Very slowly they raise up their flowers and then their bodies, and then stretch up into the sky. This symbolizes growth and new life.

3. The worship service should be a model for one's private devotions so anyone who attends even a few times can develop a viable quiet time of his own, unaided. The crisis of personal devotions comes in most cases as the result of never learning how to worship. One should get in the habit of listening to God and responding with the six various types of prayer.

    a. Worship and Praise—either use a hymn or single out a characteristic of God cited in Scripture.

    b. Thanksgiving—thanks for something God has done in your life, in the Christian community, or in the world.

229

c. Confession—should include a general confession that over against the Creator you are a "creature," as well as specific shortcomings of both commission and omission.

d. Intercession—standing before God shouldering the needs and concerns of others and presenting them to him.

e. Petition—telling God about your own needs.

f. Commitment or Consecration—the giving of oneself to God both generally and in specific commitments.

Example: PRAYER OF CONFESSION (In Unison)

Father God, we confess that we are not what we should be or could be as Your people. We are not happy about this. When we pause in Your presence, we know we need Your Spirit's work in us. Why? Because the closed mind, the stubborn attitude, and the unforgiving spirit make us too hard. Our recklessness, carelessness, and scurry after the less important have us working against You. At times we are too sensitive—at other times not sensitive enough. We sulk; we complain; we don't reach out to anyone else; we submerge in self-pity; we sit there. We don't listen; we don't speak up; we don't involve ourselves—and so we contribute to this world's troubles, and to the breakdowns between us. We know it—and we need your prompting Spirit! Hear our continuing prayer . . .

4. Worship should be the discovery of Christ with the congregation and not for them. The staff should not do all the worshiping for the congregation. Ample time should be allotted for lay participation and for spontaneous response. Further, since God dwells in each believer, He can speak through each Christian to the staff as well as through the staff.

Example: CONSUMERISM POINT AND COUNTERPOINT

Man ever finds his life in tension. Can we consume without becoming consumer-oriented? In our church life (the gathered Christians) will we merely receive and not give?

We will contract some thoughts from Scripture with how society might react.

230

In the Area of Security:

Matthew 8: 20 (RSV)—Foxes have holes, and birds of the air have nests; but the Son of man has nowhere to lay his head.
Society says: (MINISTER reading)
If you've got it, flaunt it; which is to say—if you haven't got it or aren't getting it, then you just aren't with it. Security is the name of the game, and security is money or power.
Scripture says: (NORTH SIDE of Congregation reading)
II Timothy 2: 11, 12—If we have died with him, we shall also live with him; if we endure, we shall also reign with him; if we deny him, he also will deny us.
Society says: (MINISTER)
Eat, drink, and be merry and ignore death. You only get what you take.
Scripture says: (SOUTH SIDE)
Isaiah 12: 2—Behold, God is my salvation; I will trust, and will not be afraid; for the Lord God is my strength and my song.
Society says: (MINISTER)
Don't trust anyone. Live as a practical atheist. Security is only found in what you control.

In the Area of Convenience

Scripture says: (NORTH SIDE)
Matthew 7: 13, 14—Enter by the narrow gate; for the gate is wide and the way is easy, that leads to destruction, and those who enter by it are many. For the gate is narrow and the way is hard, that leads to life, and those who find it are few.
Society says: (MINISTER)
Don't buck the tide unless it pays in money or power. You're only young once, so do your thing. Take the easy way.

In the Area of Labor

Scripture says: (SOUTH SIDE)
Ephesians 4: 28—Let the thief no longer steal, but rather let him labor, doing honest work.
Society says: (MINISTER)
You're not a thief unless you get caught. Everybody has an

angle—whether it is outright theft or just deception in use of time or resources.

5. Since our worship service is attended by people of various spiritual, social, cultural, and intellectual backgrounds, there must be special appeal for each until we go to multiple services. Each should hear his own musical sound every Sunday, if possible. Thus each service should contain classical, folk, country, soul, and Gospel song musical forms blended together in tasteful fashion. Special programs featuring one of these forms should be a regular part of our church program. Similarly, the Scripture and the sermon must contain applications relevant to these various groups. Again, individuals from each of these diverse groups should be asked to participate formally in the service. Let the church glory in the diversity of the Body of Christ as well as its unity.

Example: Spirituals from the black church, country music, selections from classics such as Handel's *Messiah,* anthems, chants from ancient liturgies, etc.

6. We should keep the basic elements of worship from service to service in order to give security and freedom to the worshiper. However, the way each is done may vary from Sunday to Sunday in order to avoid triteness and "ritualism."

Example: The Scripture reading may be read by one or more persons, dramatized by a group, sung by the choir, read with guitar or instrumental accompaniment, presented through choral speaking, read responsively between pastor and congregation or pastor and choir, accompanied by a mime, or recited antiphonally by one side of the congregation speaking to the other.

Appendix C
WORKING PAPER ON EDUCATION

Like the proverbial old gray mare, education wasn't what it used to be at LaSalle either.

> Education that is Christian will involve the whole man. Perceptions must be experienced emotionally and volitionally, creating trust and love and resulting in new values and modified behavior. Hence, a teaching of Scripture that is not internalized and applied is inadequate learning. Teaching a truth does not mean it has been experienced.

LaSalle's highly educated membership was acquainted with the latest findings by secular education.

> According to Dale's cone of learning, one remembers about 15 percent of what one hears, only about 70 percent of what he hears and sees, and about 90 percent of what he hears, sees, and does. The best educational methods involve doing (direct purposeful experience, mockups, games, dramatic participation). The next best involve observing (demonstrations, field trips, exhibits). The least effective involve symbolizing (film and recordings, visual symbols, lectures).

Example: "REAL-LIFE SAMARITAN."

The leader asks the mostly black group to pretend they are in Lincoln Park at night. The roleplaying drama begins with the mugging of a white boy by three blacks, who take his wallet and his shoes. As he lies wounded, a well-dressed white and a minister in

233

clerical collar "pass by on the other side." Then a poor Cabrini-Green black arrives, summons an ambulance, accompanies him to the hospital, and pays the emergency-room charges.

LaSalle concluded:

Formal-learning situations should be pupil centered, rather than teacher/content oriented. Further, the greatest lessons in life are caught and not taught. The life of the leader will have greater impact than anything he says. Again, as much time as possible should be spent in nonformal situations as faith is always best taught in a life context. Living together provides an ideal context for sharing God's words.

Appendix D

WORKING PAPER ON FELLOWSHIP

As believers we are part of the Body of Christ. As such, we should be a community (intimate and interdependent family) rather than a society (isolated individuals separated by basic differences despite unifying factors of mutual service rendered). Our oneness should be an experience as well as a proposition.

Oneness with our fellow Christians transcends all the differences that exist among people. It implies (1) a firm belief that God has ordained our mutual interaction to maximize spiritual growth, (2) an unconditional acceptance of each other as equals rather than as superior-inferior, (3) freedom for each other to choose our own directions or go at our own pace, allowing for diversity, and at times, conflict, and (4) a mutual sense of responsibility and accountability to each other.

Example:

Kem and Jeanie Luther's baby was born prematurely with the lung membrane deficiency which had taken the life of John and Jacqueline Kennedy's third child. The Luthers were told that their child probably would not live. They requested that Bill ask the church to pray. The first member called was a black senior citizen whom he knew to be a praying woman. "Honey, you tell the Luthers not to worry about that baby," she assured. "God won't let her be taken away. I'll pray and fast and get the other senior citizens in my building to pray with me. That baby's gonna be fine." The baby recovered.

Early at LaSalle Bill had seen that "all Christians are gifted by the Spirit for the upbuilding of the body and/or its outreach in the world." Extending this concept, LaSalle said:

> Opportunities must be provided within the structured program of the church for the discovery and affirmation of gifts and the mutual ministry of lay members as pictured by Paul's use of the Body of Christ imagery. This mutual ministry includes encouragement, listening, help in decision-making, affirmation, prayerful undergirding, sharing, exhortation, forebearing and bearing, assurance of forgiveness, and accountability.

Example:

Jerry, a young man of 21 from a poor family, an active worker at LaSalle, completed his course schedule at a Chicago Evangelical school in mid-semester and was due to graduate in May. Meanwhile, a report reached school authorities that he had let his hair and beard grow long. The tale-bearer also said he had seen a bottle of wine in Jerry's apartment. The result was that two days before commencement Jerry received a registered letter saying he could not graduate, nor could he receive a transcript. He came to Bill, who enlisted Chuck Hogren's legal counsel. Bill and Chuck talked to the dean, who showed them the school's rules against long hair, beards, and drinking. "You have no proof that he was actually drinking," Chuck said. "We feel at least he should get his transcript." When the dean refused this, Chuck threatened to file a declaratory injunction suit and give the story to the newspapers. The dean backed down and a compromise was proposed: Jerry would agree to get a haircut and shave and would be allowed to graduate.

Early in the '60s LaSalle's young adults had started cell groups. They learned through much floundering that just meeting in small groups didn't automatically produce fellowship. Their search for "meaningful meeting" led them to believe:

> Fellowship takes place in small groups when there is honest and meaningful interaction about ourselves and our relationships to God

236

and others. As Spurgeon noted, fellowship is knowing and being known; it is the mutual sharing of our inner identities and of what Christ is doing in our lives. God wills that we should know each other. The following are suggested as guidelines:

a. We must be honest in our relationships with each other.

b. Any lowering of the mask must be voluntary and not forced.

c. We are to speak the truth in love; yet, for the most part, our relationships should be pastoral and not prophetic, affirmative and not corrective.

d. Information imparted must never hurt anyone else or destroy other meaningful relationships. Confession of sin, other than strictly personal, is best confined to those who have been wronged.

Appendix E

WORKING PAPER ON EVANGELISM

The unique contribution which Christians, individually and collectively, can make in this world is to help people come to a personal relationship with God through Jesus Christ. If this be true, evangelism should always be high on the agenda of the church and the believer.

We must thoroughly grasp that the Great Commission (Mt. 28:19, 20) is to *disciple* people and not merely to convert them. Converts are to be discipled and they are expected to disciple others in the same way.

Friendship evangelism, where we share what we have experienced in Christ with neighbors, co-workers, and daily contacts, is most normal. Small groups of believers may band together in task forces to present Christ to special target groups. God may call some to a ministry of confronting strangers on the street with the Gospel. This should be done in love with respect for the dignity of strangers. However, all believers should not be browbeaten or berated for not doing the same.

The key to evangelism is to get the "body of Christ" to function as God intended.

A believer should build a special relationship with the convert, to meet regularly for prayer, to help him get started in his regular fellowship with Christ, and to see that he becomes involved in the

Body of Christ. The church should provide orientation retreats and a "School of Christian Living" for new and young Christians.

Example:

One of many persons reached through friendship evangelism was Eileen, a Ph.D. candidate in German literature at the University of Chicago. Eileen came from a prominent family in Evanston, where her father was president of the school board. She had attended church as a young girl and was having intellectual doubts about Christianity when a friend invited her into LaSalle's south-side cell group. Through the cell group she became aware of a dimension in human relationships which only Christ could offer. The cell group experiences led to a conference with Bill, after which she made a personal commitment of faith and applied for membership in the church.

Appendix F

WORKING PAPER ON SOCIAL CONCERN

True Christian social concern is of three kinds: social reconciliation, social relief (welfare) and social reform (socio-political action). By deeds of mercy, the Christian seeks to bring relief to suffering and healing to hurt. This type of action, however, does not exhaust the church's duty. Relief projects are intended to deal with symptoms. They do little to remedy the original causes of the hurt. They temporarily relieve some suffering by applying a "band-aid," but frequently do not improve the lot of the recipient. By itself it is inadequate. The basic conditions in society which generate these human problems must be reformed. The Christian must address himself to both "symptoms" and "causes" simultaneously. There needs to be a ministry to both individuals and institutions.

The church must develop a social consciousness within the church community by constant education, admonition, and encouragement in every area and age level of church life. Specific proposals should be made as to how individuals can get involved. The membership as a whole should be encouraged to participate in community organizations, volunteer services, service clubs, labor unions, political groups, and other socially oriented groups.

The church should regularly evaluate the relief needs of her neighbors and seek to creatively care by expanding existing efforts and creating new programs. One should keep in mind that in many instances, the interests of the needy are best served if the church channels its effort through existing agencies or creates inter-church

241

or inter-organizational structures to minister to these needs. In this regard, the church can recruit material resources and volunteer workers for these agencies and encourage them to function at a high level of efficiency. The church should be educated with regard to private and governmental welfare programs and be encouraged to support bona fide programs as part of its Christian obligation and witness. The church should be informed about pending social legislation on local state and federal levels.

In order to maintain the unity of the church, and due to the separation of church and state, it is probably better if the . . . church participates in social relief but not social reform. The church should instruct and inspire her members to undertake social change. Further, the church should inform her membership of on-going organizations already formed to combat a particular evil or they may even create such a group. The church does have a mission to the state. While subject to the state in so-called temporal affairs which do not involve the compromise of her unique principles, the church does have the task of nourishing, judging, and repairing the moral and political ethos of our time. The church must constantly remind the state of the disparity between the existing social order and what it ought to be. There are times when the moral mandate is so clear and the consequence to humanity so great that the church must make bold use of its prestige and power, speaking specifically to issues and programs and acting unitedly as a major block of power. Such action should be taken only upon a non-manipulated majority consensus that has been reached.

At all levels of the church structure, study groups should investigate social issues and confront the church with both a majority and a minority report. They should include an evaluation of alternatives for action. They should speak *to* the church and not *for* the church. One of the alternatives for action should be selected for implementation. The church should tolerate legitimate differences since in the present social and political milieu, choices for courses of action are often between varying shades of gray.

242